MAUNSELL LOCOMOTIVES

BRIAN HARESNAPE

AMBERLEY

First published 1977. this edition 2019

Amberley Publishing
The Hill, Stroud
Gloucestershire, GL5 4EP

www.amberley-books.com

British Library Cataloguing in Publication Data.
A catalogue record for this book is available from the British Library.

ISBN 978 1 4456 9461 0 (print)
ISBN 978 1 4456 9462 7 (ebook)

Typeset in 10pt on 13pt Sabon.
Typesetting by Aura Technology and Software Services, India.
Printed in the UK.

Contents

'King Arthur' class 4-6-0 No. 789 *Sir Guy* at speed with the 'Atlantic Coast Express' in pre-war days. Maunsell's classic development of the Urie LSWR design. (Ian Allan Library)

Foreword

Richard Edward Lloyd Maunsell, C.B.E., M.A, was trained at the Inchicore Works of the Great Southern & Western Railway, in his native city of Dublin, and gained early experience on an English and an Indian railway before returning to take charge of Inchicore. There he earned a reputation for straight speaking and dealing and as a most capable administrator. As an engineer he was a 'natural'. At the height of his career as CME of the Southern, with 15000 staff and heavy responsibilities, not least the provision of rolling stock for what became the world's largest suburban electrification, Maunsell was seen at his happiest when sauntering around the workshops, chatting with the craftsmen and handling the bits and pieces. In his dress and manner he might be taken for an old-fashioned family doctor, with starched collar and a searching gaze, quick-fire questions and positive decisions. He was explosive if provoked; encouragement he gave with a twinkle in his eye and a soft Irish brogue.

In his days at Inchicore he may well have used the Rosslare-Fishguard route to England – there were no commercial links between the GWR and the GSWR – the better to sample the sort of performance put up by Churchward's engines. To the last he was a shrewd observer of what was going on in the railway world, and at a time when four-cylinder 4-6-0s were appearing on some railways with noticeable lack of success, the Swindon version was outstanding. Ironically, Maunsell's successor at Inchicore, Watson, attempted a four-cylinder 4-6-0, which was a failure.

So it came about that Maunsell's first new design for the SECR, the N class 2-6-0 of 1917, was almost pure Swindon, with 200 lb boiler pressure, taper boiler with Belpaire firebox, long stroke and valve travel. The Ns, and later the Us with larger driving wheels, were most successful, as indeed were all his designs, except the three-cylinder Uls and the Q class 0-6-0s, which were mediocrities. He was cautious about his four-cylinder 4-6-0, *Lord Nelson*, and there was a lengthy trial period before multiplying the class. His three-cylinder 4-4-0 'Schools' proved a masterpiece.

Unfortunately, for most of his reign as a CME the capital expenditure on new locomotives was, for various reasons, restricted. Unlike his friend and contemporary H. N. Gresley of the LNER, he did not get the chance to launch a Pacific before he retired; nor could he follow the policy of the LMS after the 1923 Grouping – namely that of scrapping locomotives known to be inefficient or relatively heavy in repairs. For example, in 1926 he produced his L1 class 4-4-0, the last but one inside-cylinder 4-4-0 type built for service in England, and certainly one of the best in every respect. A mere fifteen were built for the immediate needs of the Kent lines, whereas in the long run, and with hindsight, it would have paid off to have built a hundred or more and to have got rid of the senile, slidevalve, unsuperheated, or otherwise dull 4-4-0s, which lingered on into the 1950s. Likewise, if only he had been allowed to build up-to-date branch line tank engines, BR would not have had to provide short-lived standard tanks for the Southern Region.

The fine worth of a locomotive can no more be appraised from a photograph than the character of a man. Maunsell was conscientious and painstaking, and he was not satisfied with achieving almost total reliability: he continued, right up to the weeks before his retirement, to interest himself in ways of achieving six-figure mileages between locomotive overhauls. In steam locomotive history, R. E. L. Maunsell will always be remembered for his 'Lord Nelsons' and 'Schools' classes for the Southern, but in this album Brian Haresnape has made an interesting collection of all the new, and the rebuilt, locomotives for which Maunsell was responsible over his lengthy railway career.

S. C. Townroe

Introduction

Some childhood impressions remain quite vivid with the passage of years; others fade and become unreliable – a strange mixture of fact and imagination. A chance meeting, or the rediscovery of some long-forgotten picture or document, can sometimes bring back these indistinct and confused memories into a pleasingly sharp new perspective. Just such an experience has been my pleasure whilst compiling this volume, and in the course of sifting through hundreds of pictures of Maunsell locomotives, I have acquired a new and deeper admiration for the man and his work. I must confess that, at a time when the locomotives he designed were still in service, my eyes were focused upon the more recent products of Bulleid, and later, Riddles. The boyish liking for all things new, powerful and impressive had not yet given way to the more mature respect for the works of earlier generations.

With hindsight, I realise just how fortunate I was to have seen so many SR steam locomotives in everyday service, although in the immediate post-war years many of the older types were in a sadly run-down condition. Maunsell's engines were everywhere in those days, and tended to be taken for granted as part of the scene – particularly the numerous Moguls. Happily, older enthusiasts of greater wisdom, who sported a camera as well as a notebook, were busy recording the engines I dismissed so lightly. Without their efforts I could not have produced this present work and to them all I now say a belated, but sincere, thank you.

I spent many happy hours by the lineside at Wimbledon in the early 1950s, in the company of a local group of spotters, watching steam on the Waterloo main line. The memories of busy summer Saturdays, with a seemingly endless procession of packed holiday trains interwoven into the paths of the electrics, come flooding back when I look at the pictures of 'Lord Nelsons' and 'King Arthurs' that are reproduced herein. It seemed so permanent, so infallible, and yet it has all gone! I hope the reader will share my voyage of nostalgia in the pages that follow.

In his foreword, S. C. Townroe, who was closely associated with the everyday running of the SR steam locomotive fleet, has given an excellent brief outline of Maunsell and his personality. Maunsell's early years in Ireland form the subject of the first part of this book and two Inchicore locomotive designs are ascribed to him, although his actual involvement in their overall design is a matter for debate. In the case of the solitary, powerful 4-4-0 No. 341 *Sir William Goulding*, the use of a Belpaire firebox and Walschaerts valve gear, plus an improved cab design, seems to have been Maunsell-inspired. By coincidence, when he moved to Ashford to take charge of SECR locomotive affairs he found another large 4-4-0 design virtually completed on the drawing board. Here again his hand can be detected in the improved cab of the L class and in last-minute changes to the front end, made in accordance with his experience with the Irish engine.

Between 1913 and the end of 1922, Maunsell was able to introduce three new types of locomotive for the South Eastern & Chatham, despite the disruption caused by the First World War, during which he was actively engaged on government work, both in Britain and France. The war delayed the production of his new designs, and for a period his attentions were diverted to the Association of Railway Locomotive Engineers (ARLE), who were concerned with the idea of producing a range of new standard locomotive designs for national use. The ARLE had in mind the prospect of railway nationalisation, once peace was restored, and a number of proposals were made for standard designs, which never materialised. Work on the proposed 2-8-0 and 2-6-0 types was undertaken at Ashford, to the recommendation of a select committee, which included such eminent engineers as Gresley, Churchward, Fowler and Hughes. Nationalisation was not yet on the cards, but in any case the work on standard types failed to reach completion, and the government produced a compromise plan. It was faced with the need to keep the workers at Woolwich Arsenal in employment, once the manufacture of munitions of war ceased. Accordingly, the new Maunsell 2-6-0 N class design was selected, as approximating to the ARLE version, and orders were placed for 100 sets of parts to be manufactured at Woolwich, for use in Britain's railways.

Design of the N class had begun at Ashford in 1914, but the war delayed completion of the first locomotive until 1917. It was Maunsell's practice to produce only one example of a new type until he was satisfied with the design, when further examples would follow. Maunsell had established a first-class design team at Ashford, including the Assistant CME and Works Manager G. H. Pearson from the GWR; Assistant Works Manager C. J. Hicks, from the GSWR; Chief Locomotive Draughtsman J. Clayton, from the Midland Railway, and Work Assistant H. Holcroft, from the GWR. The N class 2-6-0 was the first example of this brilliants team's approach to locomotive design and was probably the first British locomotive to have a combination of high superheat and long travel valves. There were GWR influences in the use of taper boiler, top feed and Belpaire firebox, whilst Clayton's Midland Railway background clearly influenced the outward style of the cab, tender and other mechanical parts. The mogul was totally unlike anything previously constructed at Ashford and helped to set the stage for SECR and CR locomotive practice over the ensuing 20 or more years. The design was clearly the 'modern' school, with outside cylinders and Walschaerts valve gear, and with the emphasis on accessibility rather than aesthetics; a generally similar 2-6-4T design was produced at the same time, showing Maunsell's aims towards standardisation.

One amusing insight into Maunsell's personality concerns the Wainwright H class 0-4-4T engines. Almost coincidentally with Maunsell's arrival at Ashford, there was a serious motive power shortage on the SECR. So bad was this state of affairs that the company had to borrow some engines from the Great Northern and Hull & Barnsley Railways, and Maunsell ordered a review of the existing SECR locomotive stock. He discovered that although 66 engines of the H class had been authorised, only 64 had been constructed when building ceased in 1910. He instituted a thorough search of Ashford Works and as a direct result of this action the missing parts for two engines were assembled as Nos 16 and 184, which entered traffic in 1915!

In the course of his career Maunsell made a number of proposals for locomotives, which never materialised. An early and most interesting example was whilst he was still at Inchicore, when the need arose for a large and powerful tank engine for work in the Inchicore-Kingsbridge, Dublin area. Maunsell proposed a three-cylinder 0-8-2T design, and initially this was drawn up with conjugated gear for the inside cylinder. The drawing office found great difficulty in working out the valve gear, due to the steep inclination of the inside cylinder, and this feature was discarded. Work was stopped completely by his successor, Watson, who designed instead a totally different 4-8-0T for the job. A second tank engine proposal, this time for a 2-8-0T, was prepared at Ashford in 1918, when Maunsell was looking for a suitable new type to work the heavy, short-distance London area goods traffic. This would have been a handsome outside-cylinder design with many features in common with the N class 2-6-0 and K class 2-6-4T. Other abortive proposals for the Southern Railway included a Pacific and – most surprising – a Beyer-Garratt 4-6-2 + 2-6-4T. These are discussed later.

On the formation of the Southern Railway in 1923, the locomotive stocks of the pre-Grouping constituents became Maunsell's responsibility, when he was appointed CME of the new railway. An immediate task was to bring about an interchange of locomotives from one section to another, to use them to best advantage. The design team under Maunsell were set the task of drawing up a policy for the construction of new standard locomotives to replace the multitude of types in traffic. Maunsell's policy may be summarised as follows:

1. Locomotives to be ahead of requirements so far as power was concerned, to be easy for maintenance and suitable for working on any section of the SR.
2. Types to be as few as possible, utilising standard parts where practicable, e.g. boilers, cylinders, motion, axles, axleboxess, boiler, mountings, etc.
3. Locomotives to be provided with Belpaire boiler and firebox with good grate area and heating surface, together with smokeboxes, blastpipes and ashpans of good capacity to ensure good steaming properties.
4. Locomotives to have long-lap piston valves, with extended port openings, to provide free-running locomotives.
5. Designs to be simple, with emphasis on accessibility for both fitters and footplate staff; so far as the latter were concerned full-size 'mock-ups' to be built for their inspection and comments.
6. Lubrication arrangements to be such that they were not attended to during a turn of duty.

From these principles, a series of standard designs were evolved, incorporating as many of the features listed as possible, bearing in mind the economic situation at the time. At one stage Maunsell hoped to be able to replace the majority of the pre-Grouping locomotives by nine standard types of his own. These would have employed only five patterns of boiler, and are shown in the accompanying table:

R. E. L. Maunsell's Standard Locomotive Proposals

Wheel Arrangement	Class	Traffic Type
4-8-0		Mineral
4-6-0	'Lord Nelson'	Passenger
4-6-0	'King Arthur'	Passenger
4-4-0	'Schools'	Passenger
4-6-0	H15	Mixed Traffic
2-6-0	U	Mixed Traffic
4-6-0	S15	Goods
2-6-0	N	Goods
0-8-0T	Z	Shunting Tank

The opportunity to complete this ambitious scheme was lost because of the poor economic state of the nation and the urgency with which the SR pressed on with electrification schemes. In fact, when Maunsell retired in 1937, the SR steam stocklist consisted of 1814 locomotives of more than 70 classes, and Maunsell's contribution was only 340 engines. Worse still, the average age of the fleet had risen from 28 in 1923 to 32 in 1937. However, Maunsell's engines were in the forefront of everyday operations and were a credit to the sound principles he had established at the outset.

It is not my intention to review all the Maunsell designs here, as each is dealt with in the sections that follow, but one class deserves additional scrutiny because of the very considerable controversy that surrounded it at one time. I refer, of course, to the 2-6-4T 'River' class, Nos A790–A809 and A890. On August 24, 1927 No. A800 *River Cray* was at the head of the down 5 pm Pullman car express from Cannon Street to Deal, running at speed downhill towards Sevenoaks, when (so it is believed) the flange of the leading wheel of the engine mounted the rail, taking the 'River' tank off the road at about 55 mph, close to the Shoreham Lane overbridge. Several carriages, including the Pullman Carmen, were flung against the abutments of the bridge and seriously damaged. The locomotive itself escaped with less damage, ending embedded in an embankment. Thirteen people were killed and 40 badly injured in this terrible derailment, and drastic immediate action was taken by the Assistant General Manager of the Southern, who ordered that all the 'River' tanks should be kept in their depots, as from 8 pm that evening, pending investigation.

The reason for the AGM's action was the fact that this was the fourth derailment of a 'River' tank in 1927. On March 27, the leading coupled wheels of No. A890 had been derailed for three-quarters of a mile at Wrotham and had then self-rerailed. As a result of this the class was kept off the Maidstone line until July. No sooner had they been reinstated than No. A800 was derailed at Maidstone East. Then No. A890 was again derailed whilst working the 10.51 am Charing Cross to Margate, between Bearsted and Hollingbourne. This train consisted of eleven coaches and was travelling at about 35 mph; only the Bissel truck of the 2-6-4T remained on the rails and seven coaches also came off, but luckily no one was seriously hurt. This accident took place on August 20, only four days before the Sevenoaks disaster; hence the need to look deeper into the causes, as the stability of the 'River' tanks was by then seriously questioned. In recent months there had been complaints from footplate staff about their riding qualities, and in particular about a tendency to sudden and violent rolling. As S. C. Townroe has recalled in a recent letter to the author, a popular song at the time was 'Ole Man River' and hence the engines were called the 'Rolling Rivers'. The rolling was caused by uneven track, which set the water awash in the side tanks; the leading truck with Cartazzi slide control did not exercise enough restraint.

The Board of Trade Inspector, Colonel Sir John Pringle, who enquired into the Sevenoaks derailment, wished to obtain a full and unbiased assessment of the riding qualities of the 2-6-4Ts and arrangements were made for two locomotives to be sent for running trials on the LNER main line between Huntingdon and St. Neots. This stretch of track was acknowledged to be in fine fettle and was something of a racing ground. Nigel Gresley supervised these trials, which featured No. A803 *River Itchen* and No. A890 *River Frome*, the latter, which had twice derailed on the SR, was the solitary three-cylinder K1 engine, with Holcroft conjugated valve gear for the inside cylinder. For the sake of comparison, a third SR locomotive took part in these trials; this was 'King Arthur' class 4-6-0 No. E782 *Sir Brian*. The trains hauled consisted of two coaches and the LNER dynamometer car, and both tanks were driven fast, No. A803 attaining 77 mph and No. A890 no less than 83.25 mph. On the excellent LNER track both engines ran smoothly, although No. A890 was livelier on the springs than the two-cylinder engine. The 'King Arthur' was considered superior in riding to both the 2-6-4Ts, however. As a follow-up, the Southern's General Manager, Sir Herbert Walker, requested some similar trials on home ground, and in October 1927 runs were made between Woking and Walton, on the SR Western section – with entirely different results! Nigel Gresley was again present and rode the engine footplates. The rolling experienced was frequent and severe and Gresley reported that at speeds of 70 mph or more the riding was unsafe for the quality of permanent way, which existed between Woking and Walton.

These findings, which proved that the 'River' tanks were sensitive to the inferior track of the SR, caused the company to instigate extensive track renewals and drainage improvements. This was, of course, a lengthy programme, and rather than have 21 locomotives out of use until the track was improved, the SR decided to convert them to tender engines. In any case the limited water capacity of the 2-6-4Ts had been criticised by the Running Department, and conversion to tender engines considerably widened their usefulness. In retrospect, Maunsell's design was somewhat unfairly maligned, but the decision to convert the class to 2-6-0s was probably the best answer in the long run.

The Southern inherited an extensive suburban service in and around London including some electrified routes, and this led to an early decision to electrify further sections of the three former main-line constituent companies; in fact various plans already existed before the Grouping and some were under way, but the favoured type of electrification differed. The SR settled for the third-rail 600 volt system. By 1930 the electrified route mileage had been increased to 226.5 miles, compared to 77.5 route miles in 1923; track miles increased from 240.5 to 739.5 over the same period. Maunsell's staff were called upon to design the electric multiple-unit rolling stocks, which, of course, displaced the larger and more modern classes of steam engine and resulted in the scrapping of many older tank engine designs. When Maunsell was appointed CME of the Southern in 1923, the CME of the former London Brighton & South Coast Railway was L. B. Billinton, and both he and Urie on the LSWR were retired by the new company. Billinton was only 39 years of age, compared to Maunsell, who was 54. The LBSC had produced ambitious plans for extension of their overhead-catenary 11000 volt electrification, and meanwhile relied very heavily upon a large stock of tank engines, including the huge Billinton 4-6-4TS, which Maunsell later converted to tender engines. Generally speaking, LBSCR locomotive practice did not greatly influence Maunsell, although he used a Brighton boiler when designing his Z class 0-8-0T, and at one time thought of adapting the E2 class 0-6-0T as a standard type.

I made mention earlier of some proposed SR locomotive designs, which never materialised. Taken in chronological order, the following designs were apparently considered by Maunsell, but never constructed: 0-6-0T shunter (1927); three-cylinder 4-4-0 (1928); four-cylinder Pacific (1933); mixed traffic 2-6-2 (1934); heavy goods 4-8-0 (1935); Beyer-Garratt 4-6-2 + 2-6-4 (1935) and two-cylinder 2-6-2T (1936).

The 0-6-0T would have been Y class, was intended to replace the various pre-Grouping designs and was based upon the L8SC E2 class. Economic factors led to cancellation of the plan for 105 locomotives, and when the scheme was again considered in the mid-1930s, the new diesel-electric shunter was a favoured alternative. The three-cylinder 4-4-0 would have been a most attractive engine, basically a smaller 'Lord Nelson', with Belpaire firebox and taper boiler. The decision to extend the route availability of such an engine, to include the Hastings line load gauge, ruled the scheme out in favour of an engine of reduced profile – the famous 'Schools' class of 1930. The 1928 proposal used Holcroft's conjugated valve gear for the inside cylinder, despite the troubles experienced with engines already fitted. The next abortive scheme was produced in an effort to improve upon the four-cylinder 'Lord Nelson' design, in particular for use on the Eastern section Continental trains, where the 4-6-0s had been found somewhat lacking. Only a few Pacifics would have been needed, and they proved to be too expensive to justify, but considerable work was done before the scheme was dropped. The SR Civil Engineer was largely responsible for the rejection of the next proposal of 1934 for a larger mixed-traffic engine, with 2-6-2 wheel arrangement and three cylinders, because he imposed quite severe route restrictions and queried the use of a leading pony truck on so large and heavy a design.

The next scheme, for a massive Beyer-Garratt 4-6-2 + 2-6-4T locomotive, was first revealed by D. L. Bradley in his book *Locomotives of the Southern Railway* (Part 1) and seems to have been an attempt to sell the idea by Beyer Peacock. Larger than the LMS and LNER designs, it would have had six cylinders of 16 in by 26 in; 220 lb psi boiler pressure; a length over buffers of 100 ft and a total weight in working order of 209 tons 10 cwt. The initial proposal for these engines was as an alternative to the abandoned Pacific, with the Eastern section Continentals in mind, but the Civil Engineer refused it. Next, it is alleged, the Garratt was considered for use between Basingstoke and Exeter, but the project was not pursued beyond the preliminary investigation stage and it is hard to believe that Maunsell took such an idea very seriously. The 1935 proposal for a standard heavy goods 4-8-0 was dropped because the length of train was governed by the length of sidings and running loops on the main lines, which meant that the S15 class 4-6-0 could cope with the loads involved.

In his foreword to this book, S. C. Townroe laments the fact that Maunsell did not introduce an up-to-date branch-line tank engine. In fact, Maunsell made several attempts to get a suitable design accepted for construction, but economic factors, plus the spread of electrification prevented any headway. In addition there was some opposition to the use of tank engines on semi-fast passenger duties, following the episode of the 'River' class derailments, but by 1936 Maunsell had drawings for an outside-cylinder 2-6-2T accepted, and authority for the construction of 20 locomotives. As early as 1927 a 0-6-2T design had been proposed and rejected by the Civil Engineer, and before settling for the 2-6-2T design, a 0-6-4T was considered. Sadly, the order for the new engines was cancelled in October 1936, most probably on expenditure grounds. It is worthwhile recalling that when O. V. S. Bulleid sought to provide new power for such duties, after World War II, he produced the revolutionary 0-6-6-0T 'Leader' class, with notable lack of success, and it was left to the 2-6-2T and 2-6-4T designs of H. G. Ivatt and R. A. Riddles to fill this need successfully, in the final years of steam.

In this series of pictorial histories, which already includes volumes on the designs of Stanier, Fowler and Churchward, I do not attempt to enter into exhaustive technical detail, or to include details of specific performances by locomotives. In this instance these are aspects that have been admirably chronicled over the years by experts such as D. L. Bradley (for the RCTS), O. S. Nock, S. C. Townroe and the late Cecil J. Allen. The emphasis is upon the visual, rather than the purely technical aspects of Maunsell's locomotives, and will I hope be particularly useful to the model-making fraternity. I have seen some really beautiful models, which are disfigured by error in detailing or by confusion over numbering. If the present work can assist in avoidance of such mistakes, I will be more than satisfied. Another aspect I do not dwell upon, as a rule, concerns accidents to locomotives in service, but I have made an exception in the case of the 'River' tanks, because the Sevenoaks derailment had such a dramatic impact upon their subsequent careers.

In addition to his range of standard designs, R. E. L. Maunsell was responsible for a number of rebuildings and experiments. Some are shown in Appendix 2, but in addition I would mention the experiments with steam and petrol-driven railcars and the construction by Manning Wardle of a further 2-6-2T, No. E188 *Lew*, for the narrow gauge Lynton & Barnstaple line, in 1925. At the end of each section I give details of locomotives that have been preserved. Since the onset of the wholesale withdrawal of BR steam power, the BRB and numerous enthusiast groups have performed minor miracles in preserving and restoring hundreds of engines. Examples of Maunsell's classes survive for posterity, and in some cases will see further active service. I have not illustrated these engines in their preserved state, as the general theme of these pictorial histories relates to the careers of various classes prior to the cessation of steam operations on British Railways. In the pages that follow I have endeavoured to present an unbiased and accurate record of the locomotive designs of R. E. L. Maunsell. A companion volume, *Bulleid Locomotives*, takes the story of SR steam design up to the onset of nationalisation and the final BR phase.

To two individuals in particular, I am extremely grateful for assistance, whilst preparing the manuscript, and selecting the illustrations. My dear friend Alec Swain spent many hours checking stocklists and compiling locomotive records, and Peter Winding generously supplied a large quantity of material about Maunsell's engines, from his personal collection; he also prepared a number of line drawings especially for this book. Peter Rowledge provided much valuable information about the Irish locomotives. For assistance in locating certain illustrations I am most grateful to C. P. Boocock, H. C. Casserley, A. Donaldson and S. C. Townroe. Once again, the valuable services of the Ian Allan Library and A. B. MacLeod are respectfully acknowledged, also the various public relations departments of British Rail. The line drawings include examples reproduced by courtesy of the *Railway Gazette* and Ian Allan Ltd. Without the generous assistance of all the aforementioned this work would have been incomplete, and my task would have been onerous indeed.

Brian Haresnape FRSA NDD.
Box Hill. Surrey.
January 1976.

The 'Maunsell Commemorative Rail Tour' organised by the Locomotive Club of Great Britain, seen here on one stage of its itinerary, hauled by Class U 2-6-0 No. 31639. The engine makes a fine picture as it heads down the Tooting Goods branch from Merton Park, on January 3, 1956. (Brian Stephenson)

The Maunsell Mogul family, both two-and three-cylinder versions, made a significant everyday contribution to Southern England steam operations for the best part of half a century, starting with the SECR N class introduced in 1917 and culminating in the U and U1 engines built in 1931. The 'River' class 2-6-4Ts were rebuilt as 2-6-0s in 1928 and one of these rebuilds, No. 31794 (originally 'River' class No. 794 *River Rother*), is seen leaving Honiton Tunnel with an Axminster–Exeter train. (W. N. Lockett)

Maunsell left Ireland in 1913 to become CME of the South Eastern & Chatham Railway. By a strange twist of fate, examples of his first 2-6-0 design for the SECR, the N class of 1917, found their way to Ireland and have many years of excellent service on the 5 ft 3 in gauge. These were locomotives assembled from parts supplied by Woolwich Arsenal, and the story behind these engines is told elsewhere. In spotless post-war CIE green livery, K1a class 2-6-0 No. 397 was photographed at Inchicore in 1949. Apart from a different chimney and smokebox door, the engine was still pure Maunsell and very nice to behold! (A. Donaldson)

Maunsell's contribution to the design of the classic British 4-4-0 passenger engine was remarkable. He took the late Victorian inside-cylinder concept and thoroughly modernised it, producing both new and rebuilt locomotives of truly outstanding capability. Class E1 4-4-0 (rebuilt from Wainwright E class) No. 1790 makes a splendid picture at the head of a Continental boat train in SECR days. His final 4-4-0 essay, the three-cylinder 'Schools' class, must surely rank as one of the all-time masterpieces of steam locomotive design. (Ian Allan Library)

The classic publicity photograph of 'King Arthur' class 4-6-0 No. E453 *King Arthur*, taken at Waterloo station, when the class received names. The engine is in original condition and clearly shows the particular characteristics of the batch Nos E448–E457 Maunsell had not yet introduced the modified cab, and the tender was one of the Drummond 'water-carts', with inside bearings to the wheels. In this intermediate stage the design was a mixture of Drummond, Urie and Maunsell practice. (P. F. Winding Collection)

SR publicity made the most of the fact that Maunsell's lovely four-cylinder 4-6-0 *Lord Nelson* was the most powerful express passenger engine of the day. The class was certainly one of the best-looking, in their original condition, as seen here in No. E857 *Lord Howe*, with finely proportioned parts and an excellent finish, which was achieved at the zenith of classic British steam design. (Ian Allan Library)

Maunsell considered the use of both petrol and steam-powered railcars as alternatives to locomotive-hauled stock for branch line and auto-train workings. In 1928 a petrol-engined four-wheeled railcar was purchased, and in 1933 a larger Sentinel steam railcar was obtained. This latter vehicle is seen here, at Brighton shed, whilst in use on the branch to Devil's Dyke. Five more sentinels were recommended for purchase, but never materialised. Two would have worked Staines–Ascot–Camberley–Aldershot, one Dunton–Green –Westerham and one, Horsham–Three Bridges, with one spare. The petrol railcar ended its days on the Colonel Stephens system, and the Sentinel was later condemned and left to rot in the open at Ashford. (Author's Collection)

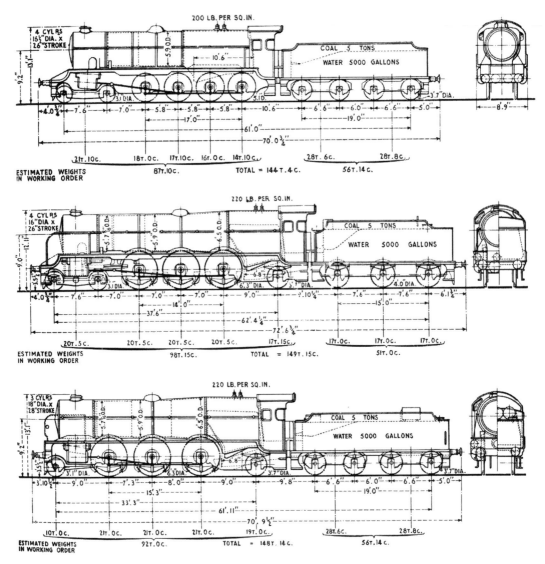

Three locomotive designs by R. E. L. Maunsell, which never materialised. (Top) The four-cylinder 4-8-0 type intended for the Kent coal traffic; (centre) the 1933 Pacific proposal for the Dover boat trains; and (bottom) the 1934 proposal for a three-cylinder 2-6-2. The Pacific had a six-wheel tender of increased capacity in order to be accommodated on existing turntables; the other two designs would have had the flat-sided bogie tenders used with the later S15s and 'Lord Nelsons'.

The ambitious Southern Railway electrification programme made heavy demands upon the CME's staff and Maunsell was closely involved in the development of rolling stock, including the express multiple-units for the Portsmouth line. He also introduced three 0-6-0 diesel-electric shunting locomotives in 1937. The mechanical parts were built at Ashford, and sent to English Electric at Preston for installation of engines and other equipment. Numbered 1–3, they became BR Nos 15201–3 in 1948 and survived in use until 1964. The first of the class is seen, when new, at Norwood Junction shed. (Ian Allan Library)

Early Days in Ireland

R. E. L. Maunsell was appointed Works Manager at the Inchicore Locomotive Works, Dublin, of the Great Southern & Western Railway in 1896, at the early age of 28. In 1911 he succeeded Mr. Coey as Locomotive, Carriage and Wagon Superintendent, a post he held for some two years before leaving Ireland to become Chief Mechanical Engineer of the South Eastern & Chatham Railway.

Section 1

4-4-0 Class 341
Express Passenger Engine
Introduced: 1913
Total: 1

Maunsell was the Works Manager at Inchicore when the proposals for a new, larger and more powerful 4-4-0 express passenger engine were made, by Coey, in 1911. Coey retired whilst the engine was still on the drawing board and Maunsell assumed responsibility for the final design and construction, almost certainly making changes. Thus No. 341 can be fairly described as Maunsell's first essay in locomotive design, although the exact extent of his influence is a matter for conjecture.

The Board decided to employ superheating for the new engine, although no superheater trials had been held by the GSWR when this decision was taken. Subsequently, an existing Coey 4-4-0, No. 326, was fitted with a superheater and 20 in by 26 in cylinders, instead of the original 18.5 in by 26 in. Maunsell's engine had a Schmidt superheater and cylinders of 20 in diameter by 26 in stroke. The firebox was of the Belpaire type, with a heating surface of 155.5 sq. ft. This, together with the tube heating surface of 1365 sq. ft and the superheater heating surface of 335 sq. ft, gave a total of 1855.5 sq. ft. The grate area was 24.8 sq. ft and working pressure was 160 lb per sq. in, although it was officially stated that this pressure could be increased to 175 lb per sq. in if the necessity arose, and in later days it ran at the higher pressure.

A technical description of the engine, published in the November 15, 1913 issue of *The Locomotive*, referred to the large increase in size and weight compared to existing engines. In fact, No. 341 was the most powerful passenger engine in Ireland when built, with the high axle loading of 19 tons 2 cwt. This confined its activities to the Kingsbridge and Cork main line. The article described the engine as the first of a new and more powerful class – thereby implying that further examples were to follow – but Maunsell's successor at Inchicore did not proceed with the design, and although O. S. Nock has written that frames were cut for more no record of this can be found in GSWR Minutes.

The design departed from existing GSWR practice in a number of respects. In particular, there was the use of the Walschaerts valve gear for the two inside cylinders; superheating; a mechanical lubricator; steam sanding; and a large improved cab with a roof, which fully covered the footplate. The platform was rasied over the coupled wheels, thereby making a welcome improvement to the task of driver's preparation. The engine was built as follows:

No. 341   Inchicore   1913

Remaining a solitary example, the engine was bound to suffer the fate of becoming nobody's concern; nevertheless it was well liked by the enginemen who worked on it.

Withdrawn: 1928

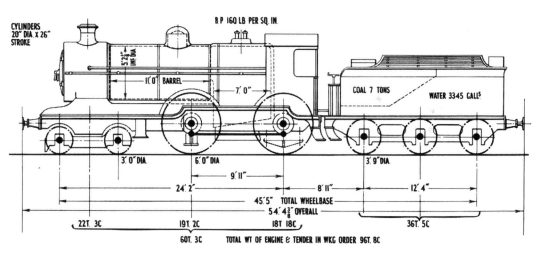

At the time of construction, No. 341 was the largest 4-4-0 in Ireland and was heavier than any 4-4-0 then running in England. The decision to name it *Sir William Goulding* after the then Chairman was taken by Maunsell and approved by the Board, although it was not the normal practice of the railway to name its locomotives at that time. The locomotive is seen here in as-built condition, in matt finish for photographic purposes. (Ian Allan Library)

The massive lines of Maunsell's 4-4-0 No. 341 *Sir William Goulding* are seen in this view of the locomotive in action. No further engines of the class were constructed by Maunsell's successor at Inchicore, although No. 341 proved a good steamer and was able to handle the heaviest trains with ease. It continued in service until 1928, ending its days as a stationary boiler at Inchicore. (Ian Allan Library)

Section 2

0-6-0 Class 257
Goods Engines
Introduced: 1913
Total: 8

In essence these rather handsome goods engines, designed during Maunsell's superintendency, were a continuation of existing practice with the important difference that they were superheated. The boiler, of round-top design, perpetuated earlier practice but the smokebox followed the practice introduced with No. 341.

The first four engines were ordered in March 1912 and had Schmidt superheaters; the second batch of four, ordered in July 1913, had an Inchicore version. Another difference was that four of them had mechanical lubricators and the other four had Detroit displacement lubricators. The tube heating surface was 844 sq. ft, the superheater heating surface was 224 sq. ft and the firebox heating surface was 118 sq. ft, giving a total of 1186 sq. ft. The grate area was 20.4 sq. ft. Working pressure was 160 lb per sq. in. The two inside cylinders were of 19 in diameter by 26 in stroke. The layout of the cylinders and valve gear were a continuation of existing practice, but a departure for goods engines was the use of 8 in diameter piston valves. Maunsell was already displaying his liking for superheating and efficient front-end design. A detail change compared to older engines of the type was the placing of the sandboxes below the platform at the front end, instead of combining them with the splashers.

The engines were built as follows:

Nos 257–260   Inchicore   1913
Nos 261–264   Inchicore   1914

Solid and reliable locomotives, they continued in use until the last days of steam in Ireland, and two even survived in store until late 1965. The boilers had been replaced by GSR N-type Belpaire superheated boilers at various times, but the original round-top boilers were also retained and refitted from time to time. During the fuel crisis of 1947 the CIE adapted the class to burn oil, and No. 264 was selected in advance of the main programme, which gives some idea of how highly the engines were thought of even at that stage of their careers.

First of Class Withdrawn: 259 (1959)
Last of Class Withdrawn: 258/60/1*/2*/3 (1963)
None Preserved

---

* Nos 261/2 stored for possible further use until 1965.

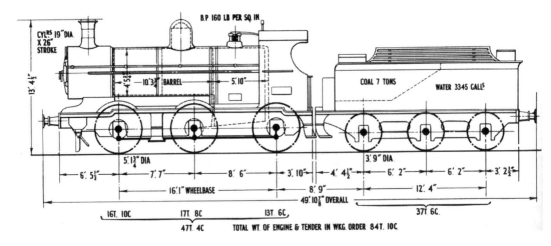

Above: In photographic grey brush, No. 260, last of the first batch of four locomotives built at Inchicore in 1913 is seen in as-built condition. A further batch of four was constructed the following year. Sandboxes for leading wheels were located below the platform. The curved handrail above the smokebox was later replaced by a straight one, on the door itself. (Ian Allan Library)

Opposite above: Fitted with an N-type GSR Belpaire superheated boiler, No. 261 was photographed in ex-works condition shunting at Inchicore on April 19, 1954. Later type of smokebox door fitted, and solid rave to the tender coal space. This locomotive, together with No. 262, remained intact until 1965, stored for possible further use, and thus survived as long as the final examples of Maunsell's Q class 0-6-0 goods engines for the Southern Railway! (R. K. Evans)

Opposite below: With a lightweight load, Maunsell class 257 (GSWR J4) 0-6-0 No. 258 makes a pleasing picture as the engine trundles through Monasterevan station. The boiler is one of the N-type Belpaire superheated boilers fitted to the class in later days. With these boilers the locomotive weight was given as 46 tons 11 cwt. The train was a Cabra-Roscrea 'Fair Special' and consisted only of a sleeping van for the crew and two brake-vans – the cattle wagons had been conveyed in advance. Photograph taken on May 5, 1957. (A. Donaldson)

Maunsell at Ashford
1914–1922

On November 12, 1913 Maunsell was appointed to succeed H. S. Wainwright as CME of the South Eastern & Chatham Railway, a position he held until the 1923 Grouping, when the SECR was absorbed into the newly created Southern Railway.

Section 3

4-4-0 Class L
Passenger Engines
Introduced: 1914
Total: 22
Wainwright/Maunsell

At the time of Wainwright's retirement, designs were in hand at Ashford for a new 4-4-0 type express passenger engine, to be built to cope with the heavy summer traffic, which was expected in 1914. Improvements to the track on the main line, over a period, now allowed a larger engine to be introduced, although Wainwright's earlier proposal for a 4-6-0 type was refused by the Civil Engineer on account of bridge loading.

On his appointment to Chief Mechanical Engineer in 1913, Maunsell found a complete set of drawings for the new 4-4-0, ready for orders to be placed. The design was prepared by Wainwright's Chief Draughtsman, Robert Surtees, but before the drawings were passed out, alterations were made to accord with Maunsell's experience in Inchicore. It is said that Maunsell sought the advice of his former Chief Draughtsman at Inchicore, W. Joynt, on such points as valve arrangements and smokebox layout. The 1.006 in lap was reduced to 0.875 in and, in consequence, reduced the valve travel. Other modifications included the provision of a Maunsell chimney, and the cab roof extended back and carried on pillars. Authority was given for 22 locomotives, straight from the drawing board, and tenders for their construction were requested in October 1913. A requirement was a delivery date in time for the summer services of 1914, and only Beyer Peacock & Co. of Gorton, Manchester; and A. Borsig, of Tegel- bei-Berlin, could meet this, so orders were placed with these two firms for twelve and ten locomotives, respectively.

The first German-built locomotives arrived in May 1914, partly dismantled, their construction in Berlin having been inspected by representatives of Messrs. Rendel, Palmer & Tritton, Consulting Engineers. Final assembly took place at Ashford, under the direction of Borsig fitters, who worked there to within a few weeks of the declaration of war. The first Manchester-built locomotives were completed in August 1914, but the last was not delivered until October. The outbreak of war prevented the new engines from being employed on the duties for which they had primarily been designed, but there was a nice touch of irony in the fact that the new German-built engines assisted Britain in the war effort!

The L class had Belpaire fireboxes; those built in Manchester had Robinson superheaters, whereas the Berlin engines had the Schmidt type. Their leading dimensions were as follows: cylinders 20.5 in by 26 in; coupled wheels 6 ft 8 in; coupled wheelbase 10 ft 0 in; boiler pressure 160 lb psi; heating surface 1412 sq. ft; superheat 256 sq. ft; grate area 22.5 sq. ft; total weight of engine in working order 57 tons 9 cwt; tender capacity 3450 gallons of water; and 4 tons of coal. Total weight of engine and tender, in working order, was 97 tons 15 cwt.

The engines were built as follows:

Nos 772–781	Borsig	1914
Nos 760–771	BeyerPeacock	1914

When new they were sent to Bricklayers Arms, Cannon St, Dover and Hastings depots, and proved invaluable for handling the heavy troop specials to and from the Channel Ports.

On the formation of the SR in 1923, the class was renumbered A760–A781; in 1931 they became Nos 1760–1781. All survived to be taken into BR ownership in 1948 and were then renumbered 31760–31781. May 1949 found them still allocated to Tonbridge, Stewarts Lane, Ashford, Ramsgate and St. Leonard's depots. In December 1951 the class began to disperse to other parts of the Southern Region, with Nos 31770–9 going to Eastleigh to take over duties of former LSWR 4-4-0s. They were, in turn, replaced by the BR standard Class 4 2-6-0s, and Nos 31776–8 were at Brighton early in 1956, working to Tonbridge, Bournemouth and Salisbury. Others remained on their home territory until the Kent Coast electrification brought about their demise.

First of class withdrawn: 31769 (1956)
Last of class withdrawn: 31768 (1961)
None preserved

L class 4-4-0 No. 760, first of the Beyer Peacock batch of locomotives, with Robinson superheaters, delivered between August and October 1914. When new, the Ls were in a simplified version of the Wainwright Brunswick green livery, without the polished brass and copper of former days. Later they carried the drab wartime grey, with large white numerals on the tender. Maunsell was almost certainly responsible for the improved style of cab used, which was similar to that on his 4-4-0 *Sir William Goulding*. (Ian Allan Library)

The volunteer foot plate men who worked on L class 4-4-0 No. A763 during the period of the General Strike painted the name *Betty Baldwin* very neatly on the leading splasher. This unofficial name remained on the engine for some months, as seen here. Photographed at Hastings on July 31, 1926. (H. C. Casserley)

Section 4

2-6-0 Class N
Mixed-Traffic Engines
Introduced: 1917
Total: 80

The outbreak of World War I seriously delayed the production of the first of Maunsell's new locomotive designs for the SECR. The design work had started early in 1914, but it was not until July 1917 that the prototype 2-6-0 No. 810 was completed at Ashford. The broad principles of Maunsell's approach to modern steam locomotive design were revealed in the stark form of the new Mogul and in the basically similar 2-6-4T, described in section 5. Nothing like these two new designs had been seen at Ashford before and the transition from the artistic inside-cylinder designs of the Wainwright/Surtees era to the functional outside-cylinder designs of Maunsell was dramatic indeed, despite the delays.

The prototype engine, finished in the austere grey livery of the period, ran trials between Ashford and Tonbridge (where it could not be accommodated on the turntable) and was then allocated to Bricklayers Arms for the heavy Richborough goods traffic, which until then had required double-heading. Trials over the rest of the SECR system followed, which certainly proved the Mogul superior to the Wainwright C class 0-6-0s and the rebuilt Stirling 01 class 0-6-0s. So successful was the design that, following the abortive attempts by the Association of Railway Locomotive Engineers (ARLE) to produce new standard locomotives to be used by British railways as a whole the Government decided to use the N class drawings – which approximated to the proposed new standard 2-6-0 – to keep Woolwich Arsenal employed once peace was restored.

This was not a productive period for locomotive building at Ashford, and some three years spanned the completion of the prototype, No. 810, and the second engine, No. 811, which appeared in June 1920. These were followed by others, numbered up to 825, which appeared in December 1923, with the exception of No. 822, which was built as a three-cylinder engine in 1922, and classified N1. The Woolwich Arsenal engines were produced as complete sets of parts between 1920 and 1922. The initial order was for 100, intended for the newly nationalised railways. However, the outcome of the political negotiations proved to be the grouping of lines into the Big Four and not nationalisation. The new companies did not take up the option, and work came to a standstill at the former munitions factory. A total of 119 boilers were supplied, from North British (85), Robert Stephenson (20) and Kitsons (fourteen), the latter ordered by the SECR. Eventually the Southern Railway purchased 50 sets of parts, which were erected at Ashford in 1924/5. Further sets of parts were purchased by railways in Ireland and by the Metropolitan Railway. The 50 Woolwich engines were numbered A826–A875 in the SR list. A further fifteen engines were built by the southern in the period 1932–4, bringing the total to 80, these latter engines having a number of detail alterations.

The design was essentially for mixed-traffic duties, with taper-boiler, top feed, high working pressure and (most significantly) long-lap valves. The Maunsell superheater was introduced with No. 810 and the top feed was of his design, housed in a dome-shaped casing. The leading dimensions of the new Mogul were as follows: cylinders 19 in diameter by 28 in stroke; coupled wheels 5 ft 6 in diameter; boiler pressure 200 lb psi; heating surface 1525.6 sq. ft (comprising a tube heating surface of 1390.6 sq. ft and a firebox heating surface of 135 sq. ft); superheat 203 sq. ft later 285 sq. ft; grate area 25 sq. ft. Outside Walschaerts valve motion was used, for ease of maintenance. Tractive effort was 26000 lb.

The engines were built as follows:

No. 810	Ashford	1917
Nos 811–815	Ashford	1920
Nos 816–821	Ashford	1922
Nos A823–A825	Ashford	1923
Nos A826–A875	Woolwich Arsenal/Ashford	1924/5*
Nos 1400–1414	Ashford	1933

The Woolwich engines were sent to the west of England when new, for use on both passenger and goods trains. The Maunsell N class proved a most useful type on all three sections of the Southern Railway, and were frequently to be seen on the cross-country routes or with through trains from the other main-line systems. In World War II the Moguls handled some formidable loads and ran extremely high mileages between general repairs. After nationalisation the design was updated, with new draughting and cylinders, but only selected engines received these modifications before the planned demise of steam brought all such expenditure to a halt.

First of Class Withdrawn: 31409/14 (1962)
Last of Class Withdrawn: 31408 (1966)
Example Preserved: 31874

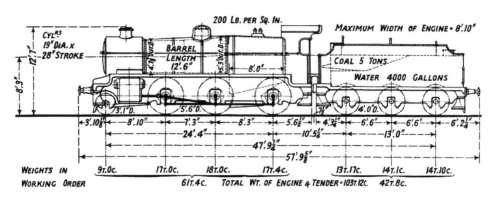

The drawing depicts one of the final series of SR-built engines with 4000 gallon tender. The original SECR drawing, with 3500 gallon tender, gave the engine weight in working order as 69 tons 8 cwt, and the tender 39 tons 5 cwt, giving a total weight of 98 tons 13 cwt. The overall length of engine and tender was given as 57 ft 6.375 in.

---

* Date of completion and entry into SR service. The sets of parts were made some two years earlier, at the Woolwich Arsenal.

The austere grey livery favoured by the SECR in World War I, and retained in post-war years, somehow emphasised the modern functional appearance of the pioneer Maunsell Moguls. No. 814, constructed in November 1920, is seen in original condition. The taper-boiler was domeless and what appeared to be a dome casing in fact housed Maunsell's top-feed apparatus. The design of cab and tender echoed Derby practice, whereas the boiler, front end, and overall basic conception was clearly Swindon-inspired. (Ian Allan Library)

In 1921 a stovepipe chimney was fitted to No. 812 in the course of a visit to Ashford for repairs, and Nos 817/9 were similarly fitted when new. Later, the stovepipe chimney of No. 819 found its way to No. 818, seen here. This ugly chimney design was not perpetuated, and was replaced on these engines by 1926/7. One point of interest is that the piston tail rods of No. 818 had been removed, although the engine is still in SECR grey livery. (Ian Allan Library)

A Worthington feed pump was fitted to No. A819 at Ashford in late 1924 and the engine ran in this experimental condition for some two and a half years. A large-diameter Maunsell chimney was used to replace the stovepipe chimney originally fitted, which was then placed on No. A818. As first built, the N class did not have footsteps at the front end; these were added later. (Ian Allan Library)

The batch of engines assembled at Ashford Works, from parts purchased by the Southern Railway from Woolwich Arsenal, were numbered A826–A875, and appeared in 1924–25. These 50 engines had boilers built by the North British Locomotive Company. The subsequent history of the remaining sets of Woolwich parts is dealt with in the introduction. Class N 2-6-0 No. A868, of the Woolwich batch, is seen when new in green livery and with the A prefix to the number. The original slender chimney is fitted, together with the piston tail rods and snifting valves on the smokebox. No. A866 of this batch was given a special finish, and exhibited at the 1925 Wembley British Empire Exhibition. (Ian Allan Library)

A private syndicate sponsored the fitting of steam condensing equipment, at Eastleigh Works to No. A816, with a view to using the equipment abroad. Invented by a Glasgow marine draughtsman, Mr Anderson, it involved extensive alterations and a year's work before the engine was ready for trials. Over the next three of four years a few abortive test runs took place, plus lengthy returns to the shops for further modifications, the engine finally being laid aside until reconversion to a normal N class took place, in mid-1935. No. A816 is seen at Eastleigh, during the experiments, fitted with a square chimney, which was later replaced by one of more conventional shape. (W. C. Casserley)

From 1933, smoke deflectors were added to the N class as they passed through the works for repairs. No. 1824 is seen soon after receiving the deflector plates, still carrying the original chimney and piston tail rods. The hand holds in the deflector plates are circular and located high up, whereas most engines had rectangular cutaway holds, lower down. The Mogul was photographed at Hither Green shed, in admirably clean condition. Note the footsteps added to the front end, behind the bufferbeam, a feature applied to all engines of the class in SR days. (Ian Allan Library)

A further experiment was applied to a member of the N class, in 1933, when No. 1850 was modified at Eastleigh with Marshall valve gear. Soon after return to service the engine became a total failure near Woking whilst working a trial trip on a Basingstoke–Waterloo train. The valve gear was considered unsuitable for the higher-speed range of passenger workings, and the engine was despatched to Brighton works for reconversion to Walschaerts valve gear, as a standard N class, in April 1934. (Ian Allan Library)

A final batch of 15 Cass N 2-6-0s was completed at Ashford Works in 1932–33, and numbered 1400–1414. These had larger, 4000-gallon tenders with turned in tops to the sides, U1-type chimneys and no piston tail rods. The engine weighed 61 tons 4 cwt in working order, and the tender weighed 42 tons 8 cwt. Nos 1407–1414 entered traffic fitted with smoke deflectors, and were arranged for left-hand drive. This superb picture of No. 1412 at the head of a breakdown train, taken when the engine was some four years old, shows also the flatter dome cover used on this batch, and the additional slidebar for the crosshead. (British Rail SR)

No. 1831 was included in the short-lived oil fuel conversion programme after the Second World War. Still in wartime black livery, with yellow lettering and green shading, No. 1831 is seen in steam at Eastleigh on September 20, 1947. Two more of the class were to be converted, Nos 1830/59, but all conversion work stopped before they could be dealt with, and No. 1831 was restored to coal burning at Ashford in the following year. (H. C. Casserley)

Ten Pullman cars make a prestige load for N class 2-6-0 No. 31407 at the head of the up 'Kentish Belle' near Herne Bay. This was an Ashford turn on Saturdays only, and presumably the Mogul was the best available power they could supply. During World War II, the Ns were to be seen on formidable loads of up to 15 or more coaches, laden with troops, often on the difficult cross-country Reading–Redhill line. They were tough and willing little engines, much liked by SR enginemen and were used on a wide variety of freight and passenger duties. (P. Ransome-Wallis)

No. 1410 of the final Ashford-built batch was fitted with smoke deflectors having a top extension, a feature it retained until BR days, when as No. 31410 the engine is seen crossing the River Thames, on the West London Extension Railway Battersea Bridge, with a through Birmingham–Brighton and Hastings train on June 18, 1949. These left-hand drive engines (Nos 1407–1414) were given new 4000 gallon tenders with the fireman's fittings correctly arranged in 1937/38. The tenders originally used were designed for right-hand drive engines. (C. C. B. Herbert)

Under BR auspices a programme of re-cylindering was introduced from 1955 onwards. In some cases completely new frames were also fitted, while in others only the front end was renewed. The new cylinders had outside steampipes and anti-vacuum valves (hidden by running-plate). The first engine to receive this pattern of cylinder was No. 31848, at Ashford in October 1955, and for some fourteen months afterwards it ran without smoke deflectors, as seen here, at Tonbridge on November 3, 1956. The program continued until 1961, by which time 29 engines had been dealt with. The new frames were higher at the front, and were curved on top, between smokebox and bufferbeam. (P. J. Abbott)

View of No. 31412, taken at Stewarts Lane. Worthy of note is the BR standard class four chimney. These chimneys were fitted to many of the re-cylindered engines, from 1957, but in addition eighteen class N 2-6-0s received new blastpipes and BR chimneys, without receiving new cylinders or frames, as seen on this particular locomotive. (M. York)

Section 5

2-6-4T Class K
Passenger Tank Engines
Introduced: 1917
Total: 20
'River' Tanks

Coincident with the design work on the N class 2-6-0, Ashford was drawing up the plans for a six-coupled express passenger tank engine. This design was also delayed by the First World War, and the prototype of the K class 2-6-4Ts, No. 790, did not appear until June 1917, actually preceding the 2-6-0 design by some weeks. In essence the design was a tank engine version of the N class 2-6-0, but with coupled wheels of 6 ft diameter as against the 5 ft 6 in of No. 810.

The appearance of the tank engine aroused very considerable interest in railway circles, as the concept was not a common one of that period and was certainly a novelty for Ashford. The use of outside cylinders with Walschaerts valve gear and a layout generally similar to the 2-6-0 gave the new engine a very modern appearance. The boiler, motion and cylinders were identical with the N class, and gave an early indication of Maunsell's aim towards standardisation.

No further engines were constructed during SECR days, partly because of the disruptive conditions of war and its aftermath. (In fact only fourteen engines were built by Maunsell entirely to his own designs during his ten years at Ashford.) The prototype was thoroughly tried and tested and found to be generally successful, although water shortage was sometimes experienced on the longer runs, such as the up 8.10 am Folkestone–Cannon Street Pullman, where a stop was sometimes required for water at Tonbridge.

In the first months of the newly formed Southern Railway, No. 790 was once again thoroughly tested and orders were placed in 1923 for 20 more engines, to be built at Ashford, with boilers obtained from Woolwich Arsenal and originally built by North British Locomotive. In the event Ashford could not find room to erect the new engines and nine sets of parts were sent to Armstrong, Whitworth & Co., for assembly, and ten sets to Brighton. The final engine of the order for 20 was redesigned as a three-cylinder 2-6-4T and classified K1; this is described in section 10.

The engines were built as follows:

No. 790	Ashford	1917
Nos A791–A799	Armstrong Whitworth	1925
Nos A800–A809	Brighton	1926

The SR decided to name the entire class after rivers; No. 790 became No. A790 *River Avon* in 1925, with the new engines being named as built.

Some modifications were made to the springing on Nos A791–A809, compared to the prototype, in particular the use of laminated springs to the bissel truck and bogie, and the use of increased superheat. The limited water capacity continued to be a source of worry to enginemen on the longer runs, particularly in the winter months. A more serious complaint, as events proved, became manifest after the class had been in traffic for some time, when footplatemen began to experience bad riding in the form of a sudden and violent rolling. In the introduction, I have examined the unfortunate episode of derailments with the 'River' class, and it is not necessary to repeat the story here, except to say that matters came to a head with the derailments of No. A800 *River Cray* near Sevenoaks on August 24, 1927 whilst working the 5.00 pm Cannon Street–Deal Pullman express. As a consequence of this fourth and most disastrous derailment, the entire class was withdrawn from traffic pending investigation. The decision was finally taken to convert the class to 2-6-0 tender engines, commencing with No. A805 in January 1928, and their subsequent history can be found in section 14.

Entire Class Withdrawn for Conversion (1927)

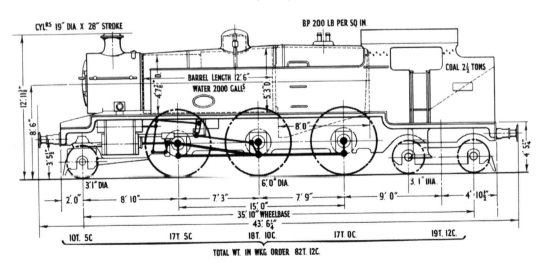

The drawing depicts the prototype engine, No. 790. Tractive effort was 23866 lbs.

Maunsell's prototype K class 2-6-4T No. 790, completed at Ashford in June 1917 and destined to remain the sole example of the class to run in SECR days. This remarkably handsome, modern design was closely akin to the N class 2-6-0s, except for the coupled wheel diameter of 6 ft, compared to 5 ft 6 in for the tender engines, an increase in diameter, which made the tank engine ideal for passenger duties. As such it was the forerunner of many similar locomotives produced in Britain, culminating in the BR standard engines of the 80000 series. No. 790 is illustrated in as-built condition. (Ian Allan Library)

In the austere SECR grey livery, without lining, No. 790, the first of the K class 2-6-4Ts, nevertheless makes an imposing picture. Orders for a further twenty engines were placed by the Southern in 1923, following extensive trials with the prototype, one of which was completed as a three-cylinder version. Nine engines, Nos A791–A799, were erected by Armstrong Whitworth & Co.; and ten, Nos A800–A809, at Brighton works; both batches had boilers built by the North British Locomotive Company, originally supplied to Woolwich Arsenal. (Ian Allan Library)

The lined green Southern Railway livery added both colour and dignity to Maunsell's tank engines, whilst the publicity decision to name the class after rivers was a pleasing touch. Detail differences, compared to No. 790, included double slide bars, regulator in the dome, increased superheating and altered springing to the bogie and bissel truck. Nos A791–A799 were fitted with Westinghouse brake equipment for service on the Central Section express workings to Brighton and Eastbourne, as seen here on No. A799 *River Test*. Standing outside Victoria station 'The Rivers' proved superior to the LBSCR Baltic tanks on the Central Section duties. (Ian Allan Library)

No. A803 *River Itchen*, standing at Redhill on October 2, 1926. When completed at Brighton, all the batch, Nos A800–A809, were allocated to Redhill and worked to Reading, but later they were dispersed to other sheds, including Dover and Ashford. This particular engine was only two months old when this picture was taken and was destined to run as a 2-6-4T for only a further ten months before withdrawal for conversion to a 2-6-0 tender engine of the U class, following the decision to abandon the 2-6-4T concept. (H. C. Casserley)

A superb camera study of Maunsell 'River' class 2-6-4T No. AB01 *River Darenth*, working the heavy through Birkenhead–Dover train, composed of both SR and GWR stock. Drivers reported a tendency for the engines to roll when on indifferent track, and there was some dislike of the class on the Central Section as a result. Subsequent trials showed that they rode well if the permanent way was in good fettle, but the conversion to tender engines went ahead. Certain parts of the K tanks, discarded when conversion took place, were later used in Maunsell's W class 2-6-4T goods engines. (M. W. Earley)

Section 6

2-6-0 Class N1
Mixed-Traffic Engines
Introduced: 1922
Total: 6

Maunsell decided to apply a three-cylinder layout to one of his N class Moguls, using the conjugated valve gear designed by his assistant, H. Holcroft, to operate the valve of the centre cylinder. The locomotive appeared in the last month of the SECR's existence, with three cylinders, 16 in by 28 in. Other leading dimensions were the same as those of the N class, but the weight was increased to 62 tons 15 cwt for the engine in full working order. The prototype was classified N1, but numbered 822, within the N series.

The three-cylinder layout permitted the use of smaller outside cylinders and the N1 design was thus suited to the London – Hastings line, where they were permitted through Mountfield and Bo Peep Tunnels, where the N class was prohibited.

Experience with the Holcroft conjugated gear eventually led Maunsell to the decision to use three sets of valve gear for three-cylinder engines, and in due course he modified No. 822 accordingly. A further batch of five N1s appeared in 1930 and these had the three sets of Walschaerts gear from new. No real long-term advantage was found in the use of three cylinders, when compared to the two-cylinder N class engines, although the N1s ran somewhat more smoothly. All the engines entered BR stock in 1948 and continued to work a variety of duties, in common with the other Maunsell Moguls.

The engines were built as follows:

No. 822   Ashford 1922
Nos A876–A880   Ashford 1930

Entire class withdrawn in November 1962.
None Preserved

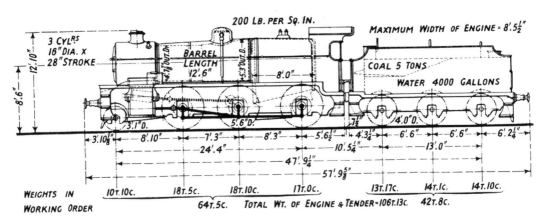

The drawing depicts one of the later engines, with three sets of Walschaerts valve gear and a 4000-gallon tender. The prototype engine, No. 822, with Holcroft's conjugated valve gear for the inside cylinder, differed in weight. The engine weighed 62 tons 15 cwt in working order, and the tender (of 3500 gallon capacity) weighed 39 tons 5 cwt. Overall length was 57 ft 6.625 in. The boiler pressure of the prototype was 180 lb per sq. in, later raised to 200 lb. Tractive effort was 27700 lb.

Although numbered within the N class series, No. 822 was classified as an N1, and it was completed at Ashford in December 1922, just before the Grouping. Because of this, it was finished in SECR grey livery, complete with cabside ownership plate. The provision of a third, inside cylinder necessitated structural alterations to the front end, which rose vertically, flush with the bufferbeam, to meet the straight running plate. The chimney fitted was of larger diameter than the N class, and part of the Holcroft conjugated gear was clearly visible, carried forward from the outside motion. No. 822 is seen at work on a goods train at Grove Park on May 10, 1924. (H. C. Casserley)

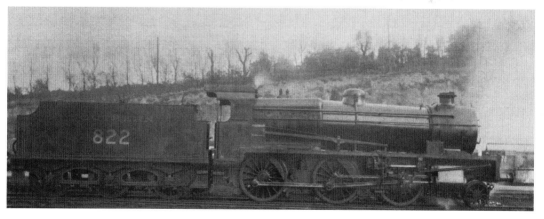

No. A822 received Southern Railway green livery in 1925, and at the same time the boiler pressure was raised to 200 lb per sq. in. The engine retained the conjugated valve gear until 1931, when it received a major overhaul and three sets of Walschaerts valve gear. The SECR ownership plate was still on the cabside when this picture was taken. No front footsteps were applied to this engine whilst carrying the Holcroft valve gear for the inside cylinder. (Ian Allan Library)

A further five N1 class locomotives were built at Ashford in 1930 and numbered A876–A880. These had three sets of Walschaerts valve gear, smaller N class chimneys, dome-mounted regulators, and 4000-gallon tenders with flat sides. Front footsteps were provided immediately behind the bufferbeam. (Ian Allan Library)

The appearance of the class was not altered much over the years, except for the provision of smoke deflectors, U1 class chimneys, and the removal of the smokebox top snifting valves. No. 31877 is seen at Argos Hill (Rotherfield) with the 4.10pm Tonbridge – Eastbourne train on July 29, 1961. (S. C. Nash)

In lined black BR livery, but without emblem or lettering on the tender, No. 31880 was photographed at St Leonards in October 1949. In BR days they worked both passenger and freight turns and were often to be seen on the numerous holiday weekend excursions, where their small wheels proved no hindrance to attaining a good turn of speed. (P. F. Winding)

Section 7

4-4-0 Class E1
Passenger Engines
Introduced: 1919
Total: 11
(Maunsell rebuild of Wainwright Class E)

The decision taken in 1917 that the post-war Continental expresses would all be concentrated upon Victoria, running via the Chatham section, presented Maunsell with a problem, because the L class 4-4-0s were too heavy for the route, whereas the lighter D and E class Wainwright engines were not sufficiently powerful for the 300-ton trains envisaged. He solved the problem by rebuilding an E class engine, No. 179, with new 19 in by 16 in cylinders, 10 in piston valves, an enlarged Belpaire firebox, top feed, superheater and improved cab.

The need to keep weight down was a paramount feature of the design, and all surplus metal fittings and ornamentation were removed. The original frames and boiler barrel were retained. The total adhesive weight of No. 179 in rebuilt form was 33.5 tons compared to 34 tons 18 cwt for the original E class. Following a trial period, from which the rebuild emerged with success, a further ten engines were similarly modernised. The dimensions of the E1 class were as follows: cylinders 19 in by 26 in; coupled wheels 6 ft 6 in diameter; boiler pressure 180 lb psi; tube heating surface 1149.85 sq. ft; firebox heating surface 127.1 sq. ft; Superheat 251.0 sq. ft; and grate area 24.00 sq. ft. Tractive effort at 85 per cent boiler pressure was 18411 lbs.

The engines were rebuilt as follows:

No. 179	Ashford	1919
No. 19	Beyer, Peacock & Co.	1920
No. 67	Beyer, Peacock & Co.	1920
No. 160	Beyer, Peacock & Co.	1920
No. 163	Beyer, Peacock & Co.	1920
No. 165	Beyer, Peacock & Co.	1920
No. 497	Beyer, Peacock & Co.	1920
No. 504	Beyer, Peacock & Co.	1920
No. 506	Beyer, Peacock & Co.	1920
No. 507	Beyer, Peacock & Co.	1920
No. 511	Beyer, Peacock & Co.	1920

For their size, the Maunsell rebuilds were truly remarkable engines and were great favourites with many enginemen, even in their later days. Outwardly they had considerable similarity to their contemporaries on the Midland Railway, but in service they had a sparkle and zest, which the Derby engines could not match, thanks to the excellent front end arrangement produced at Ashford.

First of Class Withdrawn: 31163(1949)
Last of Class Withdrawn: 31067 (1961)
None Preserved

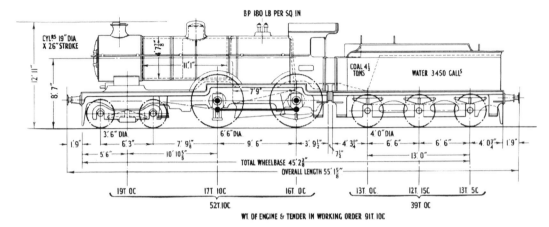

The drawing depicts the first engine to be rebuilt.

As many N class details as possible were incorporated in the rebuilt 4-4-0s, and the overall design was intended to keep weight down to the minimum. The splashers were as narrow as possible and the whole engine was devoid of any unnecessary ornamentation, thereby producing a very workmanlike appearance in striking contrast to Wainwright's artistic and graceful original design. First of the E1 rebuilds was No. 179, which appeared from Ashford in 1919. Ten more followed in 1919/1920; these were rebuilt by Beyer Peacock. No. 504 is illustrated, in SECR livery, in original condition with top feed and Ramsbottom safety valves. (Ian Allan Library)

No. A163 makes a fine study, working a down main line train past Knockholt station signal box, in the summer of 1926. Details to note include the Beyer Peacock worksplate below the smokebox saddle, the steam reverser and the fluted side rods. No steam heating hose was fitted during the summer.

Another view of E1 class 4-4-0 No. A163, at Stewarts Lane, whilst temporarily converted to an oil-burner. This took place during the 1926 coal strike and four of the class were equipped, (Nos A19, A163/5, A179) for a period of some five months. Earlier, in 1921, No. 165 had run as an oil-burner for a short period. (Ian Allan Library)

The top feed apparatus was removed from the E1 class boilers in SR days, and the boilers were also interchanged with the smaller D1 class engines. An increase of weight became possible after 1923 and Maunsell added to the weight on the coupled wheels by replacing the original cast-iron drag boxes and certain other items, which had been removed when converting the engines from Wainwright's design. Their weight in working order then became 53 tons 9 cwt. Class E1 4-4-0 No. 31067 is the train engine, with class D1 4-4-0 No. 31749 as pilot, on this p.w. special working, photographed en route from Bat and Ball to Tonbridge, at Hildenborough on November 4, 1961. (S. C. Nash)

Section 8

4-4-0 Class D1
Passenger Engines
Introduced: 1921
Total: 21
(Maunsell rebuild of Wainwright Class D)

So successful was the rebuilding of selected examples of the Wainwright E class that Maunsell turned his attention to rebuilding some of the smaller D class in similar manner, when more powerful engines were needed for the Chatham line business expresses and the accelerated Kent Coast workings. The design was basically similar, except that the D1s had 6 ft 8 in coupled wheels, a shorter coupled wheelbase, side feed to the boiler, flat side rods, and were slightly lighter. The weight in full working order was 51 tons 5 cwt for the engine, later increased to 52 tons 4 cwt when track improvements had been made on the Victoria – Bickley section of the Chatham line.

The dimensions of the D1 class engines were as follows: cylinders 19 in by 26 in; coupled wheels 6 ft 8 in; boiler pressure 180 lbs psi; tube heating surface 1276.98 sq. ft; superheat 228,0 sq. ft; grate area 24.0 sq. ft. Tractive effort at 85 per cent boiler pressure was 17950 lb.

The engines were rebuilt as follows:

No. 145	Ashford	1922
No. 246	Beyer, Peacock & Co.	1921
No. 247	Beyer, Peacock & Co.	1921
No. 470	Ashford	1926
No. 487	Beyer, Peacock & Co.	1921
No. 489	Beyer, Peacock & Co.	1921
No. 492	Ashford	1927
No. 494	Beyer, Peacock & Co.	1921
No. 502	Beyer, Peacock & Co.	1921
No. 505	Ashford	1927
No. 509	Ashford	1927
No. 545	Beyer, Peacock & Co.	1921
No. 727	Ashford	1922
No. 735	Beyer, Peacock & Co.	1921
No. 736	Ashford	1927
No. 739	Ashford	1927
No. 741	Ashford	1927
No. 743	Ashford	1927
No. 745	Ashford	1927
No. 747	Beyer, Peacock & Co.	1921
No. 749	Beyer, Peacock & Co.	1921

In terms of everyday performance these rebuilds proved to be equally as successful as the E1s, and both classes did great work before the advent of the 'King Arthurs' on the Continental boat trains. Even in their final years they performed in outstanding fashion when handled by keen footplatemen. The two classes can fairly be described as among the more brilliant of Maunsell's locomotive designs, only to be eclipsed in the 4-4-0 category by the same designer's later 'Schools' class engines.

First of Class Withdrawn: 1 747* (1944) 31 736 (1950)
Last of Class Withdrawn: 31 749 (1961)

None Preserved

---

* No. 1747 was withdrawn in October 1944 after air-raid damage.

Locomotives for the Southern Railway 1923–1938

R. E. L. Maunsell was appointed to the post of Chief Mechanical Engineer of the newly formed Southern Railway in 1923. The SR was an amalgamation of the LSWR, LBSCR, SECR and railways of the Isle of Wight and the Lynton & Barnstaple Railway. Maunsell assumed responsibility for the locomotive requirements of a system of about 2160 route miles, with major locomotive workshops at Eastleigh, Brighton and Ashford. The Southern Railway took over 2285 locomotives, made up of 125 different classes, with an average age of 28 years, and Maunsell hoped to replace a large proportion of these with nine standard types. This ambition was not fulfilled for reasons largely beyond his control, as discussed in the introduction. The true measure of Maunsell's services to steam locomotive engineering in this final phase of his active career can be appreciated only when it is realised that his achievements were made against a background of continuous and widespread expansion of electrification, and spanned a period of serious economic depression.

The Eastleigh Transition – Urie to Maunsell

Before describing the new locomotive designs produced by Maunsell for the Southern Railway, a brief pictorial summary of the 4-6-0 designs of R. W. Urie's big engine policy for the LSWR is presented, to illustrate the transitional phase at Eastleigh, when Maunsell was considering the adoption of Urie's designs for wider use.

R. W. Urie had initiated a sound policy of standardisation, with large engines of rugged and simple two-cylinder design, with outside cylinders, Walschaerts valve gear and high running plates for maximum accessibility. They were thoroughly workmanlike engines, with a rather austere appearance, but not always reliable steamers. At the time of the Grouping Urie was 68 years of age and due to retire. A building programme was under way at Eastleigh, based upon an estimate of new locomotive needs given to the LSWR Directors in 1919. This had included more engines of the three types of 4-6-0: the N15 class express passenger, the H15 class mixed-traffic and the S15 class heavy goods. Maunsell agreed to the continuation of much of this programme when he succeeded Urie, and sought ways to improve their steaming, also adding his own superheater as time progressed.

Two of the three Urie 4-6-0s were selected by Maunsell for further construction: the N15 and the S15. He redesigned the front-end layout to Ashford principles, thereby greatly enhancing their performance, and modified their overall dimensions to give them a wider route availability. These later Maunsell engines are described in section 9 and section 13. The illustrations that follow depict the original Urie types, and include various minor changes made by Maunsell over the years.

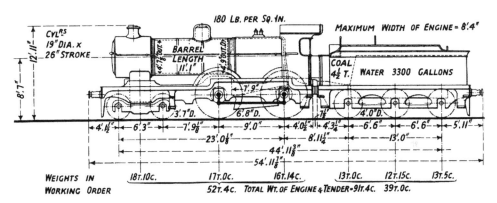

The D1 class rebuilds had side feed boilers, and when first delivered the engine weight in working order was 51 tons 5 cwt. The drawing shows the weight as increased after 1923.

In 1921 Maunsell commenced rebuilding some of the smaller Wainwright D class 4 4-0s along similar lines to his highly successful E1s. Ten engines were sent to Beyer Peacock and later a further eleven were rebuilt at Ashford, in the period 1922–1927. One of the earlier Beyer rebuilds is seen here, in SECR livery, as No. 247. Apart from the side feed boilers, the D1s differed from the E1s in having flat side rods, and they retained their 6 ft 8 in driving wheels and shorter coupled wheelbase. (Ian Allan Library)

The 'Night Ferry' sleeping car train, in full cry, double-headed by D1 4-4-0 No. 1487 and an L1 class 4-4-0 (see section 11). The contrasting chimney styles of the two classes are well illustrated, as are the different tenders used. No. 1487 has pop safety valves fitted in place of the Ramsbottom type, and steam heating for the sleeping cars, even in summer. (Ian Allan Library)

An attractive scene, with D1 class 4-4-0 No. 31727 coupled to a former SECR Birdcage brake carriage, and passing beneath the signal box at Tonbridge yard, on empty stock duties. Very little alteration was made to the appearance of these smart engines during their lifespan, apart from livery changes. In final days they ran in the lined black BR livery, and were still kept in clean condition, being highly regarded by many enginemen. (P. Ransome-Wallis)

Class D1 4-4-0 No. 31489 on the Hawkhurst branch with a special train conveying pupils from Benenden Girls School on April 5, 1960. The engine is seen entering Horsmonden station. This was the only regular working for a 4-4-0 on the branch at that time. The engine still carried Beyer Peacock works plates below the smokebox saddle, and apart from the removal of the smokebox sniffing valves was still in original condition externally. (Derek Cross)

The first Urie 4-6-0 design to appear on the LSWR was the H15 class mixed-traffic class, with ten engines built at Eastleigh in 1914. These had 6 ft diameter coupled wheels. One of the 1914 engines is seen here in BR days as No. 30485, photographed at Eastleigh in May 1954. Apart from the addition of smoke deflectors (by Maunsell) the appearance of the engine had scarcely altered in forty years. It was withdrawn from traffic in April the following year. (A. R. Carpenter)

Urie's handsome two-cylinder express passenger 4-6-0 design, the N15 class of 1918, was an advanced concept for its lime, with a taper boiler, raised running plate, Walschaerts valve gear and stovepipe chimney. Everything about Urie's engines was keyed to accessibility and ease of maintenance, and their construction was robust. In everyday service the N15s were unreliable steamers although they had plenty of power and a good turn of speed. Maunsell set about improving their steaming, and also selected the design for further building in an improved form. The engines became part of the 'King Arthur' class, and were greatly improved. No. 744 (later to become *Maid of Astolat*) is seen in original Urie form at Waterloo, in LSWR green livery. (Ian Allan Library)

Urie had a second batch of ten, improved H15 class 4-6-0s authorised at the time of the Grouping, although Eastleigh had not started to assemble them. The order was approved by Maunsell and Nos E473–E478 and E521–E524 appeared in 1924. Maunsell did not alter the design, except to provide No. E524 with an Ashford-type superheater, and later to apply his own style of chimney in place of the original stovepipe. The N15 coned boiler was used, and the running plate was straight and high enough to clear the coupled wheels. Vacuum pumps were fitted, working off the left-hand crosshead. The tenders were of Urie design, with a capacity of 5000 gallons. Total weight of engine and tender in full working order was 136 tons 7 cwt. (Ian Allan Library)

Prior to the Grouping, Urie had decided upon the reconstruction of the five Drummond F13 class four-cylinder 4-6-0s, which were dismal performers. He envisaged a drastic alteration, along the lines of his earlier Drummond rebuild, the two-cylinder H15 No. 335 of 1914, and as such they also would be virtually new engines. Maunsell agreed with this scheme, and in 1924 Eastleigh commenced the work. Little of the Drummond design was retained, except the old boiler shells, the eight-wheeled tenders and the bogies. Maunsell superheaters were fitted, but there is little doubt that the majority of the design work was to Urie's specification. The engines were numbered E330–E334. (Ian Allan Library)

No. 30333, in BR lined black livery, carrying the later Maunsell additions of smoke deflectors and lipped chimney. These Drummond 'rebuilds' were easily identified by the huge smokebox front, with relatively small door. The engine is seen working an evening freight for Salisbury, leaving Eastleigh on July 3, 1956. It was withdrawn from service two years later. (C. P. Boocock)

The third of R. W. Urie's outside-cylinder 4-6-0 designs for the LSWR was the S15 class, with 5 ft 7 in coupled wheels, intended for heavy goods traffic. These were introduced in 1920, and had a similar boiler to the N15, but pitched lower. No. 30512 is seen in BR days, at Eastleigh in April 1959, virtually unchanged in appearance except for Maunsell chimney and smoke deflectors. (C. P. Boocock)

Class H15 4-6-0 No. 522, after fitting of smoke deflectors and Maunsell chimney, seen on a Bournemouth train, at Worting Junction. By 1934 many of the Urie engines had been fitted with Maunsell superheaters, as seen here on No. 522, with the snifting valves visible on the smokebox. The crosshead vacuum pumps were removed from all the Maunsell and Urie engines originally fitted as they proved expensive to maintain. (M. W. Earley)

When the need arose to provide a spare boiler for the original Urie H15 series. Nos 482-491, Maunsell decided against building one to the 1914 pattern. In 1927 he therefore fitted a coned N15 boiler, complete with Ashford superheater, to No. 491. This released the original boiler for repair and further use, as a spare for the other nine engines. The Maunsell boiler remained with the engine, into BR days. It is seen here as No. 30491 on a Waterloo-West of England train, passing Basingstoke, in August 1949. (R. F. Roberts)

Section 9

4-6-0 Class N15
Express Passenger Engines
Introduced: 1925*
Total: 74
'King Arthur'
Urie/Maunsell

The original design, by R. W. Urie, appeared from Eastleigh in 1918 and was basically an express passenger version of his H15 class mixed-traffic 4-6-0, which he had introduced in 1914. Urie used a more efficient coned boiler and larger coupled wheels of 6 ft 7 in diameter, but the general layout was the same, with two outside cylinders and Walschaerts valve gear. The new engines were designated N15 class and 20 were built in LSWR days, numbered 736–755. In service they failed to live up to expectations, and were steam-shy when being worked hard. An early move was made by Maunsell to discover the causes of the bad steaming and he also examined the overall design with a view to improving it.

---

* Original Urie design was introduced 1918. Total includes Urie locomotives as modified by Maunsell.

There was an urgent need for more big engines in 1923 on the newly formed Southern Railway, and the traffic manager was already talking in terms of locomotives capable of working loads up to 500 tons at a start-to-stop average speed of 55 mph. Maunsell was authorised to proceed with the design of an entirely new engine, which eventually materialised as the four-cylinder 'Lord Nelson' class. Meanwhile the new company was faced with an immediate engine shortage, particularly over the former LSWR main line. This need could not be delayed whilst a completely new design went through all the intricate stages of design, construction and testing. Maunsell, therefore, decided that an improved version of Urie's N15 class would suit his purpose. He found that, prior to Grouping, an order had been given to Eastleigh works for the rebuilding of the four-cylinder Drummond 4-6-0s Nos 448–457 as two-cylinder engines. Nothing had been done, however, and Maunsell was able to alter the order and obtain authority to replace the Drummond engines with completely new N15 class engines, which would only utilise the tenders and bogies, and sundry small items, from the Drummond class, which could thus be retained in traffic until the very last moment.

For the new N15s Maunsell instructed his Ashford draughtsmen to remodel the front end layout with a new cylinder design, long-travel valves and a higher boiler pressure. Whilst this work was in hand he turned his attention to the 20 existing Urie N15s, and by less extensive modifications to the front end he succeeded in making them steam properly. These modified Urie engines had a subsequent performance, which was much improved, if not quite the equal of their later brethren, and were incorporated into the 'King Arthur' class when the SR publicity department decided to name their new express passenger engines; in some cases they carried the new nameplates whilst still in their original condition.

The new batch from Eastleigh took the numbers of the Drummond engines they were replacing and they were built to the LSWR loading gauge, with high arched cab roof. Even before the first engine was complete, the SR had decided to order more of the class to meet the traffic needs of the 1925 summer service. Time was short, and it was decided to order 20 engines from the North British Locomotive Company, in the hope of having some at least ready in time. Ordered in December 1924 the first appeared in May 1925 – a truly remarkable effort by the contractors! The design was further modified by Maunsell for this batch, using an Ashford-style cab, which brought the class within the composite loading gauge and allowed their use on the lines of the former SECR and LBSCR, with certain exceptions. Further orders, during 1925/26, brought the total of new N15s to 54, including Nos E793–E806 built at Eastleigh with smaller six-wheeled tenders for use on the Central Section. A fifteenth engine of this batch was authorised, but not built, becoming instead No. E850 *Lord Nelson*.

The original LSWR batch of Urie-built N15 4-6-0s had the following dimensions: cylinders 22 in by 28 in; coupled wheels 6 ft 7in; boiler pressure 180 lb psi; tube heating surface 1716 sq. ft; firebox heating surface 162 sq. ft; superheat 308 sq. ft; grate area 30 sq. ft. Tractive effort was 26200 lb. Weight in working order was 77 tons 17 cwt for the engine and 57 tons 1 cwt for the massive 5000-gallon tender, giving a total weight in working order of 134 tons 18 cwt. The Maunsell version of the design, in the form constructed by the North British Locomotive Company, had the following dimensions: cylinders 20.5 in by 28 in; coupled wheels 6 ft 7 in; boiler pressure

200 lb psi; tube heating surface 1716 sq. ft; firebox heating surface 162 sq. ft; superheat 337 sq. ft; grate area 30 sq. ft. Tractive effort was 23900 lb. Engine weight in working order was 80 tons 19 cwt and the Urie double-bogie 5000-gallon tender was 57 tons 11 cwt, giving a total weight in working order of 138 tons 10 cwt.

Mention has already been made of the choice of names for these engines, all from the Arthurian legends. With the exception of King Arthur and Queen Guinevere the Maunsell batches were all named after various Knights of the Round Table and the Urie batch were names of persons and places associated with them. The public relations value of the 'King Arthur' class names was enormous, and did much to attract attention to the new engines, although Maunsell himself was reserved on the subject, merely observing that names would in no way improve the performance of the engines!

The engines were built as follows:

Original Urie LSWR design of 1918

| Nos | 736–745 | Eastleigh | 1918–19 |
| Nos | 746–755 | Eastleigh | 1922–23 |

Maunsell's improved N1 5 design

Nos	E448–E457	Eastleigh	1925
Nos	E763–E782	North British	1925
Nos	E783–E792	North British	1925
Nos	E793–E8O6	Eastleigh	1926/7

The illustrations that follow depict most of the detail changes that took place over the years, in particular the various smoke-deflecting devices that Maunsell tried out before finalising the quite attractive smoke deflectors, which were subsequently fitted to all the larger SR tender engines.

The careers of the 'King Arthur' class locomotives were more than a little affected by the progress with electrification on the Southern, and they were ousted from the Central section in 1933 after a mere seven years on those lines. The outbreak of World War II curtailed the electrification schemes and placed added demands on the class; it was the subsequent appearance of no less than 140 new Bulleid Pacifics that actually created redundancies. All the Pacifics were in traffic by 1951, and scrapping of the N15s began in January 1953.

The 'King Arthurs' were splendid engines, much liked by the majority of footplatemen, and their performance in everyday service was trouble free and sometimes impressive in terms of haulage capacity. For example they could be relied upon to handle loads of 400 tons at an average speed of 55 mph, over the Western Section and on the London – Brighton run they had no difficulty covering the 51 miles in less than an hour, with the heavily loaded business expresses.

First of Class Withdrawn: 30754 (1953)
Last of Class Withdrawn: 30770 (1962)

Example Preserved: 30777

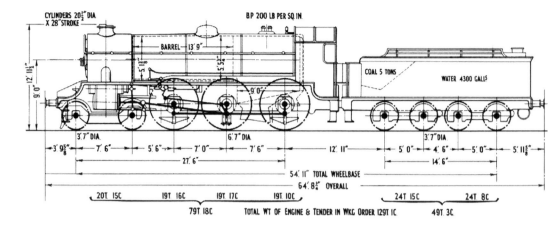

The drawing depicts the series Nos E448–E457, built to the LSWR loading gauge and fitted with Drummond inside bearing tenders.

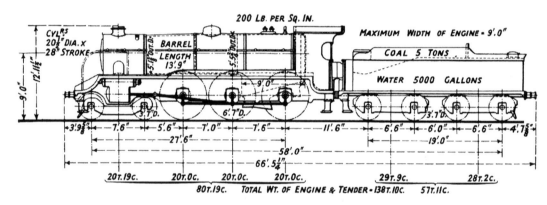

The drawing depicts the Maunsell series of 'King Arthur' class 4-6-0s, Nos E763–E792, built by the North British Locomotive with Urie tenders, and after fitting with smoke deflectors Ashford-style cab; built to composite SR loading gauge.

Opposite above: 'King Arthur' class 4-6-0 No. E452 *Sir Meliagrance*, of the batch numbered E448–E457, built at Eastleigh in 1925. The Urie-style cab was used, together with Drummond tenders, formerly attached to his 4-6-0s and refurbished by Eastleigh. This batch was built to the former LSWR loading gauge, with high arched cabs, and was therefore restricted to the Western Section of the Southern Railway. The front end was remodelled on Ashford lines, with large ports and steam chests and long travel valves, and with a decrease in the cylinder diameter from 22 in to 20.5 in. A higher boiler pressure of 200 lb per sq. in was used and Maunsell superheaters were fitted. Detail alterations, compared to the original Urie N15, design, included outside steampipes, lipped chimney and crosshead vacuum pump. (H. Gordon Tidey)

Maunsell gave considerable thought to the problems of keeping exhaust steam and smoke clear of the driver's cab, and a number of experiments were made, both on locomotives and later with scale models in a wind tunnel. No. E453 *King Arthur* is seen, whilst running in 1927 with two very small smoke deflectors fitted. Some further examples of the experimental fittings are included in the illustrations that follow. Maunsell finally arrived at a medium-sized design of smoke deflector, which was then filled to all the large SR passenger and goods tender engines, as they passed through the works. (P. Ransome-Wallis)

Smoke-deflection experiment on No. E450 *Sir Kay*, in the form of a small scoop immediately behind the chimney. The Drummond tenders attached to Nos E448–E457 carried 4300 gallons of water and live tons of coal, and weighed 49 tons 3 cwt in working order. The inside hearings on all the large Drummond tenders were a source of trouble, due to being too small for the load carried, and were prone to gel water in them. In Urie's day the tender had been redesigned with outside axleboxes to overcome this problem, and Maunsell subsequently improved the design for use on the later 'King Arthurs', S15s and 'Lord Nelsons'. (Ian Allan Library)

Another smoke deflection experiment, this time applied to one of the original Urie engines, No. E753 *Melisande*, in the form of a small curved plate across the front of the smokebox. The original Urie N15s were improved by Maunsell, with less extensive alterations to the front end, and these were then considered only slightly inferior to the later engines. No. E753 is seen after the Maunsell draughting alterations, but still carrying the Urie design of smokebox door (also a feature of Nos E448–E457 when new) and not fitted with a crosshead vacuum pump, or with Maunsell's Ashford superheater. In 1928–31 the Eastleigh superheaters on the Urie N15 boilers were replaced by the Maunsell type. (C. Riley Collection)

Nos E763–E792, built by the North British Locomotive Company, had Maunsell cabs, to comply with the composite SR loading gauge (as did Nos E793–E806 built at Eastleigh.) This permitted their use on the Central and Eastern Sections, with certain limitations. When first built, Nos E763–E792 had the large Urie double-bogie tenders fitted, as seen here on No. 764 *Sir Gawain*. Later, Nos E763–E772 received six-wheeled 4000-gallon tenders for service on the Eastern Section, and their original 5000-gallon bogie tenders were attached to S15 class 4-6-0s. Further exchanges took place in later days, including exchanges with the 'Schools' and 'Lord Nelsons', and also involved some of the later flat-sided 5000-gallon tenders, which Maunsell developed from the Urie design. (P. F. Winding Collection)

Maunsell 'King Arthur' class 4-6-0 No. E767 *Sir Valence*, on a Down Continental Boat train, at Herne Hill in 1927. The smokebox door design differed from the original Urie version, and was secured by six nuts and lugs spaced around the circumference, with no central locking device. This design later replaced the originals on the E448–E457 and E736–E755 batches, with appropriate alterations to the handrails. (P. Ransome-Wallis)

The 'Atlantic Coast Express' of 1926, speeding through Surbiton with an immaculate 'King Arthur' No. E776 *Sir Galagars* in charge. In their original condition, before the addition of smoke deflectors, the Maunsell 'King Arthurs' were extremely good-looking engines. The North British batch did not have piston tail rods fitted, and originally carried circular NBLCo worksplates on the smokebox sides, above the outside steam pipes. (F. R. Hebron)

Eastleigh produced Nos E793–E806 for use on the Central Section, and these had Ashford pattern 3500-gallon six-wheel tenders, so that weight was reduced, and also so that they could be used on existing turntables. The reduced capacity was quite sufficient for the shorter runs involved. No. E795 *Sir Dinadan* is seen leaving Victoria with a train for the South Coast, soon after entry into service. (P. F. Winding Collection)

The 3500-gallon tenders, of Ashford pattern, had higher intermediate draw gear than the Urie bogie tenders and during construction of Nos E793–E806 the rear of the engine was modified accordingly. This prevented them from running with the larger tenders unless structural alterations were made. The 'King Arthurs' with 5000-gallon bogie tenders were only permitted to work over the Central Section if they carried no more than 2.5 tons of coal and 3300 gallons of water. No. E802 *Sir Durnore* is seen at Victoria, with the small capacity six-wheel tender, and with the piston tail rods originally fitted to this Eastleigh-built batch. (Ian Allan Library)

Another of Maunsell's experimental smoke-deflecting devices in the shape of an open-ended box completely surrounding the chimney on No. E783 *Sir Gillemere*, photographed at Oxford on April 9, 1927. Both the LMS and the LNER made a series of similar smoke-deflecting experiments before concluding that Maunsell's findings were probably right. The GWR did not find the need to fit deflectors to its larger locomotives, however! (H. C. Casserley)

German-type smoke deflectors, complete with sloping front to the running plate, applied to No. E772 *Sir Percivale*, photographed at Waterloo on a Bournemouth express, in 1926. Maunsell concluded that somewhat smaller deflector plates would suffice on engines built to the British loading gauge, and the final pattern certainly looked better than the German version, whilst proving quite effective. (F. R. Hebron)

With a 4000-gallon six-wheeled tender attached, for service on the Eastern Section, No. E763 *Sir Bors de Ganis*, first of the 'Scotch Arthurs', seen at the head of a Continental Boat train. It is fitted with the final design of smoke deflectors, which had a pleasing curved aspect and which were attached to the handrails at the top. The location is Shakespeare's Cliff Tunnel, Dover. (Ian Allan Library)

'King Arthur' class 4-6-0 No. E771 *Sir Sagramore*, fitted with standard Maunsell smoke deflectors and attached to a new flat-sided 5000-gallon bogie tender, which it received in May 1930. The 4000-gallon six-wheeled tender previously fitted was then transferred to a 'Schools' class 4-4-0. Nos E763–E772 all exchanged tenders in the 1930s, in some cases with 'Schools', in others with S15s. Further exchanges took place when the 'Lord Nelson' class received the flat-sided tenders in 1932 from Nos E768–E772. The one illustrated here was then attached to 'Lord Nelson' No. E859 and the 'Arthur' received an earlier Urie pattern 5000-gallon tender in exchange. (Ian Allan Library)

In November 1940, 'King Arthur' class 4-6-0 No. 783 *Sir Gillemere* was fitted with three stovepipe chimneys set triangularly on the smokebox, with the apex to the rear, in an attempt to make the exhaust less visible from the air. Low-flying German aircraft found steam locomotives very easy targets to spot and there had been instances of trains being shot up. Any method of dispersing the exhaust to the atmosphere more speedily was considered worth attempting, but the experiment on No. 783 was not a success. A second stage of the experiment is seen here, at Eastleigh on January 7, 1941, when the engine had two chimneys, the centre one having been removed. One bad side effect was that the exhaust dislodged large amounts of soot from tunnel walls! In 1942/3 the LNER borrowed Nos 739/40/2/4/7–51/4 for use in the North East and Scotland. (B. W. Anwell)

With the exception of No. 755 *The Red Knight*, all the Urie batch had the cylinder diameter reduced to 20.5 in, and from 1932 to 1934 Maunsell further improved Nos 740/3/5/6/8/52 with double exhaust-ported steam valves. In 1940–41, Bulleid fitted an improved pattern to Nos 738/50/1/5. A multiple jet blastpipe and chimney was fitted by Bulleid to No. 755 in 1940 and this engine proved to be an exceptional performer in this condition, with original cylinder diameter of 22 m retained. Nos 736/7/41/52 also received multiple-jet blast pipes, and it was intended to fit further engines, but wartime conditions prevented this. Nos 736/52/5 had vertical smoke deflectors fitted. No. 792 of the Maunsell engines also received a multiple-jet blast pipe and chimney in 1940. No. 755 *The Red Knight* is seen here in Malachite green livery. (P. F. Winding Collection)

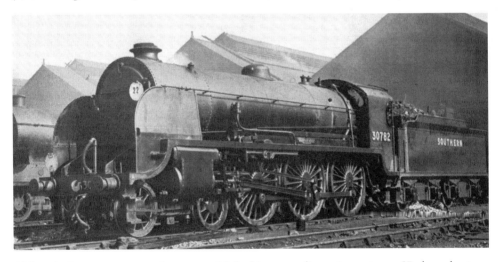

Although there was a general return to Malachite green livery in post-war SR days shortage of paint led to a few engines being repainted in the plain black of wartime. One example was 'King Arthur' 4-6-0 No. 782 *Sir Brian*, painted black at Eastleigh in 1947, and renumbered as BR No. 30782 in 1948, still in black livery. The smokebox top sniffing valves are still in place, although by this time Bulleid had removed them from most Maunsell engines. (W. Gilburt)

Two 'King Arthurs' received spark-arresting chimneys of particularly unattractive fabricated design in an attempt to reduce the number of lineside fires caused by the enforced use of poor quality coal and consequent spark throwing. No. 784 *Sir Nerovens* was fitted from June 1 947 to May 1948, and again from February 1949 to October 1954, and is seen here at Eastleigh on June 12, 1949 in Malachite green with BR numbering. The other engine fitted was No. 30788 *Sir Urre of the Mount*, from January 1950 to June 1951. The steaming of these engines was somewhat affected, although the spark-arresting device was effective, and no further such experiments were made with the class. The shape of these chimneys gave the engines the nickname the 'Beefeaters'. (W. Gilburt)

No. 30740 *Merlin*, of the original Urie N15 series, seen here in BR dark Brunswick green livery with orange and black lining, at Eastleigh on May 28, 1950. The engine has electric lighting, which was fitted in 1947 whilst the engine was running as an oil-burner. Ten N15s were selected in 1946/7 for conversion to oil fuel, but only five were dealt with before the scheme was abandoned. These were Nos 740/5/8/9752 and were all returned to coal-firing in the autumn of 1948. They retained the electric lighting that had been fitted whilst they were oil-burners, and also the tubular steel ladders at the rear of the tenders. (W. Gilburt)

No. 30453 *King Arthur* leans to the curve on the down main line through Clapham Junction, in BR days, still attached to a Drummond water cart tender. By 1955 some of these tenders were in very poor shape and withdrawals commenced, with the engines receiving newer Urie bogie tenders instead. The Urie series of N15s were all withdrawn from traffic in the mid-1950s, but some of their tenders lived longer, attached to Maunsell 4-6-0s. (P. F. Winding)

No. 30457 *Sir Bedivere*, photographed at Nine Elms on October 24, 1959 with the Urie bogie tender off H15 class 4-6-0 No. 30490, in place of the Drummond water cart inside bearing version, which was originally fitted to the 448–457 batch of 'King Arthurs'. Apart from various minor modifications the class remained substantially as built throughout the whole of its existence, until these tender changes were made. (C. P. Boocock)

The last 'King Arthur' class 4-6-0 to remain in service on BR was No. 30770 *Sir Prianius*, which survived in steam until November 1962. The engine is seen in its final BR condition taken from the window of an electric train running in the same direction on an adjacent track as it passes Queens Road, Battersea. Under normal service conditions the 'Arthurs' could always be relied upon to handle loads of up to 400 tons, at an average speed of 55 mph, on the Western Section – sometimes exceeding this standard of performance – throughout their lengthy career in main line service. (P. F. Winding)

With a standard of cleanliness every bit as good as the best of pre-war days, 'King Arthur' class 4-6-0 No. 30796 *Sir Dodmas le Savage* makes a splendid picture, leaving Cannon Street with the 5.47pm to Ashford and Dover on May 30, 1958 – the last week of steam operation before the introduction of diesel electric multiple units. Following this, the engine was transferred to the Western Section, losing the six-wheeled tender seen here for a 5000-gallon Urie tender. (R. C. Riley)

No. 30806 *Sir Galleron*, photographed
at Eastleigh on July 21, 1959, attached
to the Urie 5000-gallon tender from
N15X class 4-6-0 No. 32331. The
valance of the engine cab footplate is
higher than the tender valance, and
required structural alteration to the
intermediate draw gear, which had
been designed to match the Ashford
type 3500-gallon six-wheeled tenders
originally fitted to Nos 793–8061.
(C. P. Boocock)

Section 10

2-6-4T Class K1
Passenger Tank Engine
Introduced: 1925
Total: 1
'River' Tank

It was typical of Maunsell's thorough approach to locomotive design matters that he
should decide to apply the Holcroft conjugated valve gear for three-cylinder engines to
an example of his 2-6-4T design as well as to a 2-6-0. The engine was not completed
until October 1925, well into Southern Railway days, but it was basically a tank
engine version of the prototype N1 class 2-6-0 and had the same massive front-end
arrangement, with high running plate over the outside cylinders.

The coupled wheels were 6 ft in diameter, and three 16 in by 28 in cylinders were
fitted, with Holcroft's conjugated gear actuating the inside piston valve. The wheelbase
was the same as for the K class 'River' tanks and the weight in working order was
88.75 tons. Although numbered separately, the engine was named in the 'River' class
series, becoming No. A890 *River Frome*. The riding of the three-cylinder tank was a
source of complaint from enginemen and for some reason it seemed even less stable
than the two-cylinder version and was twice derailed, as mentioned in the introduction.
No. A890 was withdrawn, together with the other 'River' class 2-6-4Ts, following the
Sevenoaks accident and stored pending an inquiry. It later ran trials for the Board of
Trade Inspector on the LNER main line and the SR Western Section and was found to
be a lively rider, with a tendency to sudden and violent rolling on poor track. It was
then decided to convert the engine to a 2-6-0 tender locomotive, and the subsequent
career of No. A890 is described in section 15.

The engine was built as follows:

No. A890   Ashford   1925

Withdrawn for Conversion to Tender Engine: 1927

No. A890 *River Frome*, in its short-lived tank engine form; resplendent in SR green livery, with red background to the nameplates. This massive and attractive locomotive proved to be less stable than the two-cylinder 'River' class 2-6-4Ts and ran off bad track on two separate occasions. These incidents, together with the more serious accident at Sevenoaks, when No. A800 *River Cray* was derailed with the loss of thirteen lives, plus 40 badly injured, led to the conversion of all the 'River' tanks to 2-6-0 tender engines. No. A890 *River Frome* was converted at Ashford in June 1928, and in its new form became the prototype U1 class 2-6-0. (Ian Allan Library)

Section 11

4-4-0 Class L1
Passenger Engines
Introduced: 1926
Total: 15

An outstanding order for fifteen new express passenger 4-4-0 engines existed at the time of the Grouping. These were for the SECR, and were to be of similar weight and capacity to the L class. The Maunsell team would have liked the chance to completely redesign the L in the light of experience with the E1 and D1 rebuilds, but when the order was postponed by the Grouping nothing much had been done. By 1925, however, the weight of many of the fast 80-min expresses to Folkestone was on the increase and the existing L class 4-4-0s were being increasingly hard-pressed on these workings. At one stage Maunsell favoured the use of his 2-6-4T 'River' class, but their limited water capacity was against them and when a need for more powerful engines became a matter of some urgency, he was only able to modify the existing L class drawings in the time available; there was insufficient time to completely redesign the valve gear along the lines of the E1 and D1 classes.

As it was, Ashford could not undertake the work involved and the new engines were ordered from the North British Locomotive Company. The existing L class drawings, patterns and templates were used, and only those modifications that could be readily introduced were authorised, to avoid delays in construction. The fifteen new, modified L 4-4-0s were thus classified L1, and differed from the 1914 engines mainly in having smaller cylinders, higher boiler pressure of 180 lb psi, Maunsell superheaters and improved cab layout with side windows and cut-away running plates with small splashers. The valve travel was lengthened to the maximum that the existing design of steam-chest would permit and the lap was increased. The N class smokebox and chimney was used, and the flatsided 3500-gallon tenders were similar to those coupled to the Moguls.

The principal dimensions of the L1 class were as follows: cylinders 19.5 in by 26 in; coupled wheels 6 ft 8 in; boiler pressure 180 lb psi; tube heating surface 1252.5 sq. ft; firebox heating surface 154.5 sq. ft, giving a total of 1407.0 sq. ft; superheat 235.0 sq. ft; grate area 22.5 sq. ft. The engine weight in working order was 57 tons 16 cwt, and the tender weight was 40 tons 10 cwt, giving a total weight in working order of 98 tons 6 cwt. Tractive effort was 18910 lb.

The engines were built as follows:

Nos A753–A759 North British   1926
Nos A782–A789 North British   1926

In service, the L1s proved to be fast engines and able to handle the Folkestone expresses for which they were primarily designed. Although their nominal tractive effort was the same as the L class, and their boiler design was basically the same, they could be relied upon to tackle the heavier loads.

First of Class Withdrawn: 31755(1959)
Last of Class Withdrawn: 31786 (1962)

None Preserved

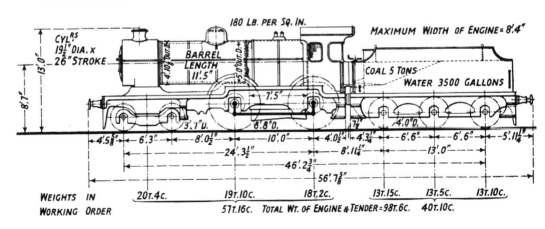

L1 class 4-4-0 as built.

L1 class 4-4-0 No. A783 in original livery with A prefix above the number on the tender. The side-window cab, flat-sided tender, raised running plate above the coupled wheels and the N class smokebox and chimney gave these engines a pleasing air of modernity. They proved to be efficient, fast and free running in everyday service and were well liked by the footplate crews. (Ian Allan Library)

The first 'Night Ferry' working took place on October 14, 1936 and the motive power was L1 4-4-0 No. 1758 and D1 4-4-0 No. 1470. The train is seen on the fourth day of working, again with No. 1758, this time double-heading an L class 4-4-0 No. 1764. An interesting photograph that affords a visual comparison between the L1 and the L class from which it was developed. The train is seen passing Bromley on October 18, 1936. (H. C. Casserley)

In full post-war Southern Railway livery of Malachite green, but renumbered into the BR series and with the tender relettered in shaded sans-serif style, class L1 4-4-0 No. 31786 was photographed on a down working near Petts Wood. All but two of the class, Nos 1753/82, ran in Malachite livery before being repainted in BR lined black and the last example in this colourful scheme was No. 31756, which remained green until mid-1953. Smokebox top snifting valves are removed, but otherwise their appearance was virtually unchanged throughout their lives. (E. R. Wethersett)

A classic picture of an L1 class 4-4-0 hard at work, in the midst of the Kentish hopfields. No. 31787, in clean BR lined black livery, is seen on an up hop-pickers special, composed of ex-SECR 'Birdcage' rolling stock, at Tudeley. Following the electrification of the Kent Coast lines the L1s were either stored or transferred to the Western Section; withdrawals commenced in 1959. (E. R. Wethersett)

Section 12

4-6-0 Class LN
Express Passenger Engines
Introduced: 1926
Total: 16
'Lord Nelson'

With the improved N15 4-6-0s successfully introduced as a stop-gap measure, to cope with the immediate need for more large express passenger engines, Maunsell was able to proceed with the requested design for a locomotive capable of working 500 ton trains at an average speed of 55 mph; these requirements had been established by the Traffic Manager in September 1923.

Maunsell approached the new design with very great care and instigated considerable investigations, before settling upon a four-cylinder 4-6-0 as the best solution. A major factor was the need to avoid any significant increase of weight, whilst producing a significant increase in power. The SR Civil Engineer had imposed a maximum axle-loading of 21 tons for the routes concerned. The final series of Eastleigh-built 'King Arthurs' had a weight of 20 tons 4 cwt on the driving axle; in other words, approaching the limit. On the 'Lord Nelson', Maunsell achieved an axle load only 7 cwt greater, despite the use of a four-cylinder layout. The empty weight of the prototype 'Nelson' was to prove only 1 ton 1 cwt greater than the 'King Arthurs', yet the tractive effort was 33510 lb, compared to 25321 lb.

In his efforts to keep down the weight of his new 4-6-0 Maunsell used high-tensile steel for the motion, which was as light as possible without sacrificing strength or durability. In the course of assembly of the prototype, No. E850 *Lord Nelson*, Maunsell had all the parts, which were normally left as forged, or cast, carefully machined to remove excess metal. Even the main frames were reduced in thickness and additional lightening holes were cut, compared to the original drawings. His aims were achieved, and in fact it did not prove necessary to take such drastic measures with the production batch, as the weight of the prototype proved to be some 15 cwt less than the drawing office estimates.

In 1924 a Drummond four-cylinder 4-6-0, No. 449, had been experimentally modified with the cranks set at 135 degrees, to give eight beats per revolution of the coupled wheels. This was claimed to give a more even torque, to reduce stress on the axleboxes and motion and to create a more even draught on the fire than was the case with quartered cranks. For the 'Nelsons', the 135 degree arrangement was used, with the drive divided between the front two coupled axles.

The principal dimensions were as follows: four cylinders 16.5 in by 26 in; coupled wheels 6 ft 7 in; boiler pressure 220 lb psi; tube heating surfaces 1795 sq. ft; firebox heating surface 194 sq. ft; superheater 376 sq. ft; grate area 33 sq. ft; tractive effort at 85 per cent boiler pressure, 33510 lb.

The grate area of 33 sq. ft was the largest of any British 4-6-0 when the class was first introduced (it was later exceeded by the GWR 'King' class) and to achieve it the Belpaire firebox was 10 ft 6 in long, 18 in longer than the 'King Arthur' firebox. The grate was in two sections, with the rear portion horizontal and the front portion steeply inclined. In the hands of an inexperienced fireman this long box could lead to poor steaming, but the 'Nelson' boiler was an excellent steam raiser when handled by men who had mastered it.

The prototype ran for some two years, on trials with service trains, whilst Maunsell satisfied himself that this very handsome engine was up to expectations, and generally reliable, before further locomotives were ordered in March 1927.

The engines were built as follows:

No. E850	Eastleigh	1926
Nos E851–E865	Eastleigh	1928/9

So much has been published already on the unexpected shortcomings of the 'Lord Nelsons', once the class was in traffic, that it is unnecessary to repeat the story here. Maunsell was aware that their performance was falling short of the standard hoped for, and indeed, he later considered an alternative Pacific design for the Continental boat trains, as mentioned in the introduction. In addition to the large grate area (which many observers believed was the chief culprit) there was the fact that only sixteen of the class were built, whereas twice that number or more would have been of greater use. Too many footplatemen were unfamiliar with their characteristics, and openly stated that they would prefer a 'King Arthur', a class which was certainly much easier on the fireman! Maunsell made a number of experiments upon individual engines, as described in the illustrations that follow, and later, Bulleid made more determined efforts to improve the class. His clumsy-looking Lemaître multiple-jet blast pipe certainly helped, and the new cylinders, with 10 in diameter piston valves, instead of 8 in, also helped to some degree.

In retrospect, the 'Lord Nelson' was an excellent machine, with many refined qualities in its overall design, and even if the sparkle was sometimes lacking, the class were remarkably trouble-free in everyday service. When Bulleid's later Pacifics were failing to provide realistic availability figures, the 'Nelsons' (albeit with Bulleid modifications) were often called upon to deputise on top-link workings; when in the hands of experienced crews, they gave their very best and harassed shed masters must have blessed the Maunsell engines! Only when BR had rebuilt sufficient numbers of the Bulleid engines with conventional valve gear was the 'Lord Nelson' class dropped to the second stream, and even then they were well maintained, and kept clean – a sure sign that shed staff appreciated them.

First of Class Withdrawn: 30865 (1961)
Last of Class Withdrawn: 30861/2 (1962)
Example Preserved: 30850

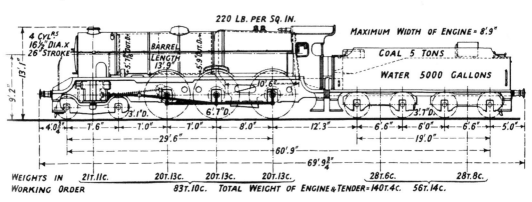

The drawing depicts a 'Lord Nelson' class engine as running with the flat-sided version of the Urie 5000-gallon tender, and with smoke deflectors added.

Britain's most powerful passenger engine – so ran the proud caption to this publicity photograph of the first 'Lord Nelson' class 4-6-0, No. E850 *Lord Nelson*, which was unveiled to the public in August 1926. It remained the sole example of the class for the following two years, whilst Maunsell had the engine thoroughly proved in everyday service. The 'Nelson' boiler design was based upon the N class 2-6-0, enlarged to the limit of the composite loading gauge. The empty weight of the engine was only 1 ton 1 cwt greater than the empty weight of a final series 'King Arthur', but the tractive effort was 33510 lb compared to 25321 lb – a very significant increase in power. (Ian Allan Library)

No. E852 *Sir Walter Raleigh*, attached to a 4000-gallon six-wheeled tender, for service on the Eastern Section, photographed soon after building in July 1928. This tender was later replaced by 'Nelson', a bogie 5000-gallon tender from 'King Arthur' class 4-6-0 No. 769; this tender had started life attached to a Maunsell S15 4-6-0! (Ian Allan Library)

Close-up of the 4000-gallon six-wheeled tender of No. E853 *Sir Richard Grenville*, photographed at Longhedge on June 1, 1929. This engine ran with the small tender from its entry into service in September 1928 until February 1930, when it received a bogie tender from an S15 class 4-6-0. A further tender exchange took place in 1932 when the Urie bogie tender was replaced on Nos 851–860 by the handsome flat-sided version, with vacuum reservoirs on the tank top. (H. C. Casserley)

For the Liverpool & Manchester Railway Centenary celebrations of 1930, 'Lord Nelson' 4-6-0 No. E861 *Lord Anson* was specially furbished and posed as No. E850 *Lord Nelson*, for exhibition purposes. This view of the true No. E850 was taken at Eastleigh in 1929 and shows the impressive appearance of the flat-sided 5000-gallon tenders, with vacuum reservoirs clearly visible to the rear of the coal space, on the tank top. Some of these tenders were originally fitted to Maunsell's batch of S15 4-6-0s and some also ran attached to 'King Arthur' class 4-6-0s for a while. (Ian Allan Library)

A classic photograph of No. E850 *Lord Nelson* at the head of the Down 'Golden Arrow', near Petts Wood, on March 27, 1931. The engine has smoke deflectors added, but is otherwise substantially as built. Maunsell made a number of experiments with members of the 'Lord Nelson' class, once the basic design had proved itself in service. In 1934 he had the cranks on No. 865 Sir John Hawkins reset to 180 deg., from the original 135 deg. No appreciable difference could be detected, but the engine, remained in the altered form – giving four exhaust beats to the wheel revolution instead of eight. (Ian Allan Library)

No. E859 *Lord Hood* was fitted with 6 ft 3 in diameter driving wheels, instead of 6 ft 7 in, to assess the performance of a smaller-wheeled express passenger engine on the more difficult SR workings. Maunsell had proposed to reduce the wheels to 6 ft diameter, to increase tractive effort, but 6 ft 3 in was the biggest reduction in diameter that could be made without considerable alteration to the frames. No marked difference in performance resulted, although the engine remained in the modified form for the rest of its career. No. E859 is seen attached to a Urie tender, working a Boat train near Dover. (M. W. Earley)

When Maunsell was considering the Pacific design for the Dover Boat trains, illustrated in the introduction, he envisaged the use of a boiler with nickel-steel plates and a combustion chamber. 'Lord Nelson' class 4-6-0 No. 857 *Lord Howe* was selected as a guinea pig and a special boiler was fitted to try out the Pacific proposals. This boiler incorporated a large combustion chamber extending from the firebox for a distance of 3 ft into the barrel and had a round-top firebox; externally it had a curious humpback appearance, with a very small dome. The length between the tubeplates was reduced to 13 ft, and the tube heating surface was therefore reduced, by 188 sq. ft. The firebox heating surface was increased by 52 sq. ft. No. 857 was photographed on March 30, 1938 passing Bromley with a Continental train. Special kinked smoke deflectors were fitted. (H. C. Casserley)

The 'Lord Nelsons' were never quite so free steaming as the 'King Arthurs', and several attempts were made to improve their draughting. The first noticeable improvement resulted from the fitting of Kylchap blast pipe and chimney to No. 862, but for some reason the application was never extended to the rest of the class. No. 862 Lord Collingwood was photographed at Nine Elms on September 15, 1934, fitted with the very distinctive double chimney design Maunsell used on these two engines. No. 865 was fitted with a similar chimney in 1938. (H. C. Casserley)

Bulleid applied his ideas on draughting to the 'Lord Nelson' class soon after he succeeded Maunsell as CME of the Southern Railway. He modified the front end, fitting all the class with Lemaitre multiple-jet blast pipes, together with a larger diameter chimney, in 1938/39. The early chimneys applied were hideous stovepipe affairs, as seen here on No. 863 *Lord Rodney*, photographed on May 9, 1939 whilst still attached to a flat-sided bogie tender, but in the new Malachite green livery Bulleid designed new cylinders for the class, with 10 in diameter piston valves instead of 8 in, and with improved steam and exhaust passages. In due course all except Nos 851/63 were dealt with. (British Rail SR)

A modification to the flat-sided version of the Urie double-bogie 5000 gallon tenders fitted to the 'Nelsons' took place in the late 1930s, and resulted in an extremely good-looking, high-sided design. The sides were raised in order to increase the depth of the coal bunker, and to induce the coal to be self-trimming. Improvements were also made to the lockers provided, to create a draught screen. The top portion of the tender sides had an inward curve to clear the loading gauge. No. 855 *Robert Blake* was photographed at Victoria, soon after receiving the self-trimming tender, and is of particular interest because it still carried the large numerals painted on the tender side after the modification, and was still in Maunsell's dark green livery. (Ian Allan Library)

Bulleids bright Malachite green livery suited the 'Lord Nelson' class well, and a nice touch was the painting of the smoke deflectors. No. 30854 *Howard of Effingham* was photographed at Eastleigh on June 12, 1949, still in pre-nationalisation colours and without emblem or lettering on the tender sides. The later version of wide diameter chimney used by Bulleid was slightly less of an eyesore than his first stovepipe affair, but still had a clumsy appearance compared to the elegance of Maunsell's 4-6-0 design as first built. With Bulleid's cylinders fitted, the outside steampipes no longer protruded through the lower portion of the smoke deflectors. (W. Gilburt)

As part of a nationwide survey of public opinion, the newly formed Railway Executive had a number of locomotives and carriages painted in experimental liveries, in the summer of 1948. The trains these engines worked were publicised, and the preferences expressed were supposed to guide the Executive in their final choice of a new livery for the nationalised rail system. 'Lord Nelson' 4 6-0 No. 30864 *Sir Martin Frobisher* was painted bright apple green, with red, yellow and grey lining, and was coupled to an eleven-coach train painted in what was unofficially described as 'plum and spill milk', which approximated to the old LNWR carriage colours. The result was not very appealing, but the final choice of red and cream was no better! No. 30864 is leaving Waterloo in the experimental livery on June 24, 1948. (British Rail SR)

A final attempt to improve the draughting of the 'Lord Nelson' class was made in 1956, when No. 30852 *Sir Walter Raleigh* was re-draughted to S. O. Ell's formula, retaining the multiple blast pipes. The engine was tilted with a squat new chimney, of the design used for the Modified Bulleid Pacifics. No. 30852 is seen leaving on the initial test run after re-draughting had been carried out at Eastleigh, with the 2.17 pm slow to Bournemouth, at Southampton Central on January 20, 1956. (G. Wheeler)

A pleasing angle to view No. 30850 *Lord Nelson*, despite the clumsy appearance of Bulleid's wide diameter chimney. The general detailing and finish of the Maunsell four-cylinder 4-6-0s was excellent and withstood the test of time extremely well. The engine was photographed at Southampton Central, awaiting the road. No. 30850 has been officially preserved, but at the time of writing was still awaiting restoration and eventual display. (Eric Oldham)

Section 13

4-6-0 Class S15
Goods Engines
Introduced: 1927
Total: 25*
Urie/Maunsell

The development of Urie's S15 class 4-6-0 heavy goods design for further construction followed much the same pattern as Maunsell had applied to the N15s. They were fitted with two 20.5 in by 28 in cylinders with long valve travel, increased boiler pressure of 200 lb psi, and Maunsell superheaters. The outward appearance was very similar to that of the later 'King Arthur' class 4-6-0s, with straight running plates, Maunsell cab and chimney.

The other leading dimensions of the Maunsell series of S15 were as follows: coupled wheels of 5 ft 7 in diameter; tube heating surface of 1716 sq. ft; firebox heating surface of 162 sq. ft; superheat 337 sq. ft; grate area 28 sq. ft and tractive effort of 29855 lb. For engine Nos 823–837 the engine weight in full working order was 80 tons 14 cwt, and for Nos 838–847 the weight was slightly less, at 79 tons 5 cwt. Tender weight varied according to the style of tender attached, but as an example, the Urie 5000-gallon tender with two four-wheel bogies weighed 56 tons 8 cwt.

The engines were built as follows:

Nos 823–837 Eastleigh   1927/8
Nos 838–847 Eastleigh   1936

The second order, for Nos 838–847, included engines for use on the Eastern and Central sections and some engines were attached to 4000-gallon six-wheeled tenders. These were the last new large engines constructed during Maunsell's term of office. The S15s were rather handsome engines and gave an excellent account of themselves in everyday service, on both goods and passenger turns, showing a lively turn of speed for a small-wheeled design. Even late on in their careers they were pressed into passenger service at peak holiday periods, whilst still tackling the heavy Western Section goods turns. They outlived the 'King Arthur' class and some were still in regular use as late as 1965.

First of Class Withdrawn: 30826 (1962)
Last of Class Withdrawn: 30837 (1966)
Example Preserved: 30841 (now named *Greene King*)

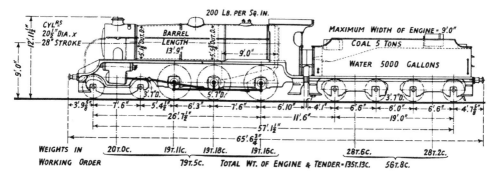

The diagram depicts one of the final engines of the batch, with flat-sided bogie tender, and fitted with smoke deflectors.

Finished in works grey livery, for photographic purposes, No. E825 actually entered traffic in goods black livery, with green lining. This was the third of the fifteen engines built at Eastleigh between March 1927 and January 1928. The Urie 5000-gallon bogie tenders of Nos E823–E832 had the turned out coal guard raves, as seen here, and weighed 57 tons 11 cwt in working order. The similarity to the 'King Arthur' class will be noted: the boilers were pitched at the same level as the N15s, and were interchangeable. (Ian Allan Library)

A really superb official Eastleigh photograph of class S15 4-6-0 No. 838, finished in full passenger green livery. The engine is attached to one of the handsome flat-sided versions of the Urie 5000-gallon tender, as developed by Maunsell, with auxiliary vacuum reservoirs mounted at the rear, on the tank top. Some of these tenders, built for the S15s, Nos 828–832, later found their way on to the 'Lord Nelson' class. Smoke deflectors were fitted to all the engines of the class as they passed through the works, as part of the general application to Maunsell's tender engines in the mid-1930s. (S. C. Townroe Collection)

Another view of No. 838, still attached to the flat-sided tender it was built with, and running as No. 838 in early British Railways livery of plain black with Bulleid-style lettering. The smokebox sniffing valves have been removed, also the crosshead vacuum pump, but otherwise the appearance of the class has remained unaltered since building. The engine was photographed on a down goods near Winchfield on April 20, 1949. At this time the engine was fitted with one of a batch of twelve new N15-pattern boilers, built by North British Locomotive Company in 1947–49. (E. C. Griffith)

Class S15 4-6-0 No. 30824 on a down Salisbury–Exeter goods near Gillingham (Dorset). The engine is coupled to a Urie-type bogie tender, and is painted in BR goods black livery. The class was never restored to the pre-war green, although they were still sometimes used on passenger duties, particularly at busy holiday periods. (W. Vaughan-Jenkins)

Nos 833–837 received 4000-gallon six-wheeled tenders from 'King Arthur' class 4-6-0s Nos 763–767 in 1936, and were then allocated to the Central Section, where the existing turntables could not take the Urie bogie tenders. No. 30835 is seen here approaching Reigate from the Guildford direction with an up freight, on September 25, 1954. (S. C. Nash)

Another tender variation on No. 30833, seen near Woking on an up stopping train from Basingstoke on a summer Saturday in July 1962. This tender was from 'Schools' class 4-4-0 No. 30908 and was attached to the S15 in May of that year. The last engine of the class to run in steam, under BR auspicies, was No. 30837, which worked a railway enthusiast rail tour to Eastleigh in January 1966, having been in store since the preceding September, when it was officially withdrawn. (S. C. Crook)

Class S15 4-6-0 No. 30845 toils up the bank to Semley with a heavy freight for Salisbury, on April 27, 1963. The engine was withdrawn from service just three months later. (A. Richardson)

Section 14

2-6-0 Class U
Passenger Engines
Introduced: 1928
Total: 50*

The Maunsell Mogul family was further developed by the design of the U class engines, with six-foot coupled wheels, intended for duties of an intermediate passenger nature, such as semi-fast and cross-country workings. The K class 'River' tanks were suitable for many of these duties, although limited by the water capacity of their tanks, but a need was felt for basically similar tender engines, and the U could fairly be described as a tender engine version of the K. At the time this decision was taken further 'River' tanks were on order and parts had been authorised, including the purchase of further boilers from Woolwich Arsenal. The unfortunate episode of derailments with the 'River' 2-6-4Ts already in service, together with the pressure of the Traffic people to have some tender engines, led to the decision to complete the order as 2-6-0s. In due course it was also decided to convert the existing 'River' tanks, although it is sometimes mistakenly stated that this decision came first. This is not so: the U class 2-6-0s were already in hand and the first engine appeared from Brighton in June 1928, although the first converted 'River' was completed the previous March, which probably explains the confusion.

The new engines were numbered A610–A639, whilst the 'River' tank conversions retained their existing numbers of A790–A809. The nameplates carried by the latter when 2-6-4Ts were removed, however, and the proposed names for additional engines were never used. In their converted form Nos A790–A809 were virtually identical to Nos A610–A639 except that their running plates were slightly lower and the smokebox saddles slightly higher. Fourteen new tenders were supplied by Armstrong, Whitworth & Co. Apart from their reduced wheelbase and larger coupled wheel diameter, the U class engines were generally similar to the original SECR N class Moguls and had many parts in common with the earlier type.

The chief dimensions of the U class were as follows: cylinders 19 in by 26 in; coupled wheels 6 ft 0 in; boiler pressure 200 lb psi; tube heating surfaces 1390.6 sq. ft; firebox heating surface 135 sq. ft; superheat 203.0 sq. ft, giving a total of 1728.6 sq. ft. Grate area was 25.0 sq. ft. Engine weight in working order was 62 tons 6 cwt, and the tender was 40 tons 10 cwt, giving a total of 102 tons 16 cwt. Tractive effort at 85 per cent boiler pressure was 23866 lb.

The engines were built, or rebuilt, as follows:

Nos A610–A619	Brighton	1928
Nos A620–A629	Ashford	1929
Nos A630–A639	Ashford	1931

---

* Total includes 20 locomotives rebuilt from K class 2-6-4T.

Nos A790–A796	(rebuilt) Eastleigh	1928
Nos A797–A802	(rebuilt) Ashford	1928
Nos A803–A804	(rebuilt) Brighton	1928
No. A805	(rebuilt) Ashford	1928
Nos A806–809	(rebuilt) Brighton	1928

The class were very successful on the type of duty for which they were intended, and although officially restricted to 70 mph maximum on passenger turns, they were steady runners and could readily exceed this speed in service.

First of Class Withdrawn: 31630 (1962)
Last of Class Withdrawn: 31639, 31791 (1966)
Examples Preserved: 31618, 31806.

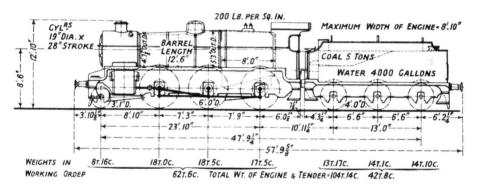

The drawing depicts the later 4000-gallon tender, delivered with Nos A630–A639 1931.

The decision to convert the 'River' class 2-6-4Ts into U class 2-6-0 tender engines was implemented in 1928, and the first example was No. A805, modified at Ashford in March of that year. Some new 3500-gallon tenders were supplied by Armstrong Whitworth & Co. In their rebuilt form the engines retained the low running plate, and consequently they had larger splashers than the rest of the class. No. A805 is seen here, soon after conversion, still with piston tail rods and original slender chimney. This engine was formerly *River Camel*. (Ian Allan Library)

No. A796, formerly *River Stour*, seen standing outside Victoria station. This was one of the ten ex-'River' tank conversions, which retained the Westinghouse air brake (Nos A790–A799,) for use on Central Section Brighton and Eastbourne trains. The cab differed from later U class engines, on these conversions, in that the cutaway portion of the sidesheets extended into the curvature of the roof, and the double spectacle plates of the 2-6-4T design were retained. (Ian Allan Library)

In original condition, with slender tapered chimney and piston tail rods, U class 2-6-0 No. A619 on a train of South Western stock. This engine would have been named *River Taw*, but the SR decided against perpetuating the 'River' class names, following the unhappy episode of derailments, and to produce Nos A610–A629 as 2-6-0 tender engines, instead of further 2-6-4Ts. The flat-sided tenders of the initial batch of U class engines had a capacity of 3500 gallons and 5 tons of coal, and weighed 40 tons 10 cwt in working order. In later years they were attached to Q class 0-6-0s, and these Us then received new 4000-gallon tenders. (Ian Allan Library)

A batch of ten engines, built at Ashford in 1931, Nos A630–A639, were delivered with larger 4000-gallon tenders, with turned-in tops. The dome cover had a latter top and no piston tail rods were fitted. No. A631 is seen, in original condition, waiting to work a Central Section excursion. (Ian Allan Library)

No. A629 was completed in December 1929, and was fitted with a German design of pulverised fuel burner. This necessitated a special tender, with a large covered hopper, which fed the fuel first via screws driven by steam, and then forced by air through piping to the firebox. The blast of air was created by a steam turbine fan, mounted on top of the tender behind the hopper, clearly visible in this view of No. A629 at Eastbourne. A secondary feed was provided, on a belt driven by steam, for lighting-up purposes. This entered the firebox at the rear, whereas the main feeds entered each side. The front of the tender had a small cab fitted. In this experimental form No. A629 was shedded at Eastbourne, where a special fuel bunker was erected, to feed the hopper from above. The engine ran trials over a period of some two years without notable success and with no fuel saving over conventional coal burning. It was an early recipient of smoke deflectors and the U1-type chimney. One failing, which did not please lineside dwellers, was a tendency to deposit large quantities of partially burnt fuel dust, still glowing, along the lineside! After a minor explosion (when it was realised that powdered coal was as lethal as gunpowder) Maunsell stopped the experiment. (H. C. Casserley)

Photographed at Willesden LMS motive power depot in 1933, class U 2-6-0 No. 1633 makes a pleasing picture, waiting to take over a through working via the West London lines to the South Coast. The piston tail rods have been removed and the 1931 renumbering applied, but otherwise the engine is still substantially in as-built condition, and has not yet received the smoke deflectors, which were applied to all the Maunsell 2-6-0s from 1933. (Ian Allan Library)

Nos 1790–95 were transferred to Yeovil in 1933, following the introduction of the 'Schools' class to Eastbourne shed, and these U class engines became very popular in the West Country, remaining at Yeovil for the next quarter of a century. Perhaps their popularity can be judged from the absolutely superb finish the cleaner has bestowed upon No. 1790, photographed at Yeovil shed. Note the burnished metal star and the immaculate smokebox trim. (S. C. Townroe)

As part of the abortive, post-war Government-sponsored oil-burning conversion programme, two U class 2-6-0s were converted to oil fuel at Ashford Works in the autumn of 1947; these were Nos 1625 and 1797. Further engines of the class were earmarked for conversion, including Nos 1629/35/7/8, and work was in hand on No. 1629 when the scheme was abandoned. Nos 1625 and 1797 operated oil-burners for a period in 1948, at Fratton and Exmouth Junction. The engines received the smaller 3500-gallon tenders (necessary in order to carry the fuel tanks within the loading gauge) and were fitted with electric lighting. No. 1625 is seen at Fratton on September 11, 1948. Livery was plain black, and by this time all the U class engines had lost their original chimneys and smokebox snifting valves. The replacement chimneys were of the U1 class pattern. (H. C. Casserley)

In May/June 1950, No. 31624 was sent to the Somerset & Dorset line for trials, to see if the class could be used to replace the Stanier 'Black Fives' on this difficult route. The engine is seen working as pilot to class 5 No. 44839 on the down 'Pines Express' at No. 2 junction, Templecombe. Tablet exchange apparatus was fitted for the trials, which were abandoned when the WR imposed 45 mph speed restriction on the 2-6-0 for their section of the route. (J. B. Heyman)

New cylinders, with outside steampipes, were fitted to engines of the class, as required, from 1955 onwards. In certain cases new frames were also supplied, but in general the renewal was confined to the front end. From late 1957 the chimney used was the BR standard pattern, but No. 31621, seen here, was the first engine to receive the new cylinders and retained the U1-pattern chimney. A total of 23 engines of the class received new front ends, in the period 1955–61. (P. Ransome-Wallis)

Some of the 'River' tank conversions were included in the U class engines, which received new front ends. By the time No. 31791 was selected, the BR standard chimney was in use for these modifications. The new framing had a graceful curve to the upper part, between the bufferbeam and smokebox. No. 31791 is seen at Shepherdswell with a weed-killing train, on May 6, 1960. The engine is fitted with BR AWS equipment, with the battery box visible on the platform, above the rear coupled wheels. (G. W. Morrison)

Some examples of the U class received new BR standard chimneys, without re-cylindering, or any other modification to the front end. No. 31793, one of the former 'River' tanks, is seen at Eastleigh on August 15, 1961, with new chimney and 25 KV overhead electrification warning signs on smoke deflectors and firebox. Note the prominent sandbox filler, ahead of the leading splasher. (G. W. Morrison)

Section 15

2-6-0 Class U1
Passenger Engines
Introduced: 1928
Total: 21

The solitary three-cylinder 2-6-4T No. A890 *River Frome* was included in the scheme to convert the 'River' tanks to 2-6-0 tender engines, and in June 1928 the locomotive emerged from Ashford, minus name, attached to a 3500-gallon tender and reclassified U1. The Holcroft conjugated valve gear to the middle cylinder was retained and the engine was very similar to the N1 class 2-6-0 No. A822 (see page 38) except the larger six-foot diameter driving wheels and shorter coupled wheelbase.

In tender engine form, the leading dimensions of No. A890 were as follows: three cylinders 16 in by 28 in; coupled wheels 6 ft 0 in; boiler pressure 200 lb psi; tube heating surfaces 1390.6 sq. ft; firebox heating surface 135.0 sq. ft; superheat 203.0 sq. ft; grate area 25 sq. ft. Tractive effort at 85 per cent boiler pressure was 25387 lb.

The Holcroft valve gear had proved troublesome on the Maunsell engines, in particular the over-running of the inside valve due to wear in the various pin joints. Maunsell was impressed by the performance of the three-cylinder version of his Mogul, in particular for its better acceleration and generally smoother running, but when further U1s were contemplated he revised the design and provided three sets of Walschaerts valve gear, later converting No. A890 to bring it into line.

The engines were rebuilt or built as follows:

No. A890 (rebuilt)	Ashford	1928
Nos A891–A900	Eastleigh	1931
Nos 1901–1910	Eastleigh	1931

The U1s were capable of a good turn of speed, and when new Nos A891–900 were allocated to Fratton for the principal Portsmouth – Waterloo services, being displaced by the arrival of the more powerful 'Schools' 4-4-0s in 1934. Their duties included many semi-fast passenger workings, and also some freights. They then went to the Eastern Section, where they did well on the summer relief trains to the Kent Coast, etc., though they did not have to produce continuous steaming throughout the journey. In the war years the class was found most useful because of their high route availability and they were in the forefront of troop train operations over the Hastings line. In later days a trial was made with one on the Somerset & Dorset line, but the locomotive tested, No. 31906, could not equal the performance of the larger engines. The official maximum speed for the U1 class was 70 mph, but O. S. Nock has published examples of runs where this speed was exceeded, with splendid sprints of up to 80 mph with loads in the region of 300 tons.

First of Class Withdrawn: 31892/7, 31902/4 (1962)
Last of Class Withdrawn: 31910 (1963)

None preserved.

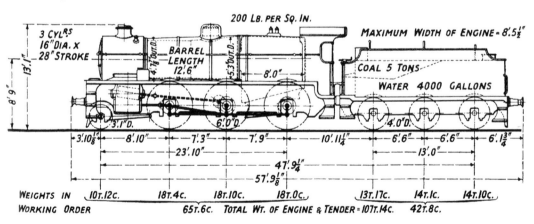

The drawing depicts the production version of 1931.

Formerly the sole three-cylinder 'River' class 2-6-4T No. A890 *River Frome*, and now rebuilt as a nameless 2-6-0 tender engine and reclassified U1, No. A890, is seen soon after conversion at Ashford in 1928. The Holcroft conjugated valve gear was retained, together with the massive footsteps to the running plate. A new 3500-gallon tender was fitted, and the cab retained the large cutaway of the tank engine, extending into the roof curvature. The conjugated valve gear was replaced by three sets of Walschaerts at Ashford in 1932. (Ian Allan Library)

Experience with the rebuilt No. A890 in passenger service led to the decision to build further three-cylinder Moguls, with 6 ft diameter driving wheels, for express working. The order for 20 more was carried out at Eastleigh in 1931 and they were numbered A891–A900, 1901–1910. The design was cleaned up somewhat, with a straight running plate, and the footsteps were moved to the front end, ahead of the cylinders; the dome casing had a flatter top. New 4000-gallon tenders were fitted, with turned in tops to the sides. Note the very small splashers above the running plate. (O. J. Morris)

Smoke deflectors were added in the mid-1930s in common with the other Maunsell Moguls, although these were of shallow depth, because of the high running plate. No. 1909 takes on an almost model-like appearance in the trim setting of Ascot station. (S. C. Townroe)

In the drab black livery of immediate post-war days on the Southern, No. 1890 makes an interesting comparison with the illustration opposite. In the intervening nineteen years between the two pictures, the engine has lost the large footsteps behind the cylinders, and the snifting valves on the smokebox top, and has been fitted with smoke deflectors. Photographed at Brighton shed in September 1947. (P. F. Winding)

Renumbered 31900 in the BR list, but still in Southern black livery, the engine makes a rousing start away from Eastbourne, with the 11.30 am through train to Birmingham New Street, on June 10, 1950. Some of the class received new cylinders in 1954, and some received BR standard blast pipes and liners without further alteration to the front end. (S. C. Nash)

Section 16

0-8-0T Class Z
Shunting Engines
Introduced: 1929
Total: 8

Designed specifically for service in the Southern Railway's principal goods yards and sorting sidings, the three-cylinder Z class 0-8-0T was the only eight-coupled Maunsell design to proceed further than the drawing board stage, although he had proposed locomotives with this wheel arrangement on earlier occasions, as mentioned in the introduction. Urie had produced the G16 class 4-8-0T in 1921 for the LSWR, with the same type of duties in mind, including hump shunting. Rather than perpetuate the Urie design, Maunsell chose to make extensive use of his own standard parts, together with an existing Brighton boiler design. The Z class incorporated a lot of features that experience with the larger Urie tanks had suggested, in particular the use of three cylinders to aid adhesion without excessive slipping, and the use of a non-superheated boiler of moderate grate area and large water and steam capacity, able to store heat for lengthy periods of waiting and to avoid excessive blowing off. Maunsell recognised that the sound of violent wheel-slip, and the roar of steam from safety valves, were not features of railway shunting operations, which endeared themselves to those members of the public living in the vicinity of marshalling yards! The Z class proved to be efficient locomotives, and very quiet in operation; although they were not found to be quite as successful for local goods duties as the Urie engines, they were extremely efficient shunters.

The leading and trailing coupled wheels were provided with sideplay so that curves of 44 chains could be negotiated, despite the wheelbase of 17 ft 6 in. Originally it was intended to use conjugated valve gear, but the Civil Engineer objected to the distance that would have resulted between the buffer face and the leading wheels. A pony truck was subsequently proposed, but not pursued, as this would have led to the loss of some adhesion. In the final design the overhang at each end was almost 11 ft, which meant that sharp curves could only be negotiated where there was ample space.

The cylinders had a diameter of 16 in by 28 in stroke, and were interchangeable with classes N1 and U1. The outside pair drove the third axle through 11 ft 6 in connecting rods, and the inside cylinder (which was set at an inclination of 1 in 8) drove the second axle. Walschaerts valve gear controlled the outside piston valves, but for the inside valve a gear designed by J. T. Marshall was used, in which a second eccentric provided the lap and lead movement.

As stated, the boiler was an existing Brighton design, of the parallel non-superheated type, and it had a heating surface of 1173 sq. ft, which, with the firebox heating surface of 106 sq. ft, brought the total evaporative heating surface up to 1279 sq. ft. The grate area was 18.6 sq. ft. Boiler pressure was 180 lb per sq. in, and tractive effort at 85 per cent boiler pressure was 29380 lb. Steam brakes were fitted, also vacuum apparatus for handling fitted vehicles, and steam heating was provided so that the engines could preheat passenger stock and banana vans.

The engines were built as follows:

Nos 950–957 Brighton   1929

A further 10 locomotives were programmed for construction at Eastleigh in 1931, but the order was cancelled due to the economic depression, and was never reinstated. Significantly, thought was being given to the use of diesel-electric shunting locomotives for such duties at about this time, and Maunsell later ordered three such engines to assess their capabilities, as mentioned on page 16 of the introduction.

First of Class Withdrawn: 30950 (1962)
Last of Class Withdrawn: 30953/4/5/6 (1962)

None preserved.

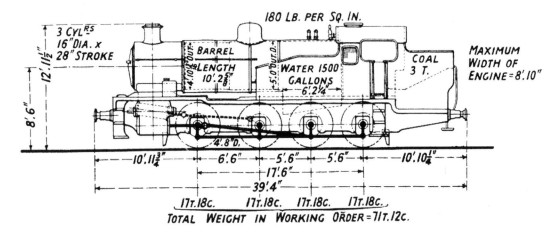

The diagram clearly illustrates the overhang at each end of the locomotive.

Class Z 0-8-0T No. 953 in as-built condition and painted in Southern Railway goods engine livery of black with green lining and yellow lettering. A steam reverser was fitted to these engines. This view clearly shows the layout of the pipes for the vacuum brake and steam heating hoses on the front buffer beam. (Ian Allan Library)

In hybrid BR livery, with Bulleid-style lettering, No. 30956 was photographed at Eastleigh in 1955. During World War II this locomotive, together with Nos 951/5, was loaned to Scotland and in 1942–43 they were reported to have been seen at various War Department areas, including Cairnryan and Stranraer. (P F. Winding)

The Brighton-built Z tanks were used at various places on the Southern system, ranging from Hither Green sidings to Exeter. No. 30952 is seen here piloting U1 2-6-0 No. 31853 on an up freight at Exeter Central. A second Z class tank was banking the rear of the train, which was photographed on September 7, 1961. The appearance of the 0-8-0Ts remained virtually unchanged throughout their career – they always looked, and indeed were, thoroughly capable and efficient machines. (G. D. King)

Section 17

4-4-0 Class V
Express Passenger Engines
Introduced: 1930
Total: 40
'Schools'

With the 'Lord Nelson' class locomotives fully established, and the 'King Arthur' class continuing to give very satisfactory service in their improved form, the Traffic Manager proposed the need for an equivalent type of locomotive for secondary services, which would be capable of hauling loads of up to 400 tons, with average speeds of 55 mph. Maunsell, therefore, at first planned to produce a smaller edition of the 'Lord Nelson', with one cylinder less and one pair of wheels less – thereby producing a relatively cheap engine to build and maintain.

Such a straightforward solution to the requirement was, however, thwarted by the subsequent decision that such an engine should be able to comply with the severe route restrictions on the Hastings main line, which already precluded the use of the two 4-6-0 classes. The Eastern Section Chatham route to Ramsgate was another which had, at that time, restrictions upon it, and both these routes were obvious choices for an engine which could comply with the restrictions and at the same time substantially improve upon existing locomotive performance.

The engines were built as follows:

Nos E900–E909	Eastleigh	1930
Nos E910–E929	Eastleigh	1932–34
Nos E930–E939	Eastleigh	1934–35

The Hastings route was the chief obstacle, because of the severe width restriction, of 8 ft 6.5 in, which required the use of specially constructed rolling stock. In particular, the narrow tunnel at Mountfield created this problem and there were also numerous severe curves on the line. Maunsell found that his first scheme, to use 'Lord Nelson' flanged plates for the shortened boiler of the proposed 4-4-0 three-cylinder engine was not practicable, because the Belpaire type of firebox did not allow an adequate cab forward look out. The Hastings line loading gauge required the width of the cab at the gutter level to be kept down to 7 ft 7 in, and the sides of the cab were turned inward from a point roughly halfway up, to provide this clearance. A round-top boiler of the type used on the 'King Arthurs' would, he realised, solve this problem and also keep weight down, although the Belpaire design would have been preferred. The new 4-4-0 therefore had the same firebox as the last series of 'King Arthurs', which had a slightly smaller grate than the original (due to the fact that a wider water-leg was used). As many other parts as possible were made standard with the 'Lord Nelsons' in order to simplify construction and maintenance.

The main dimensions of the new 4-4-0 were as follows: three cylinders 16.5 in by 26 in; coupled wheels 6 ft 7 in; boiler pressure 220 lb psi; tube heating surfaces 1604 sq. ft; firebox heating surface 162 sq. ft; superheat 283 sq. ft; grate area 28.3 sq. ft; tractive effort at 85 per cent of boiler pressure 25130 lb.

The SR publicity department, aware that considerable business was done with school traffic, and seeking names for the new class, hit upon the bright idea of naming the engines after public and private boarding schools, not only within Southern territory, but also some in other parts of the country. The new engines were, wherever possible, taken to the nearest station for exhibition to the boys, and a great deal of goodwill was generated – besides the novelty of seeing the class in areas which they did not normally visit.

Without doubt these 4-4-0s must rank as Maunsell's masterpiece, and might justifiably be described as the finest engines of the wheel arrangement ever to run in Britain. They were excellent steamers, good to handle, and capable of performances more in keeping with the expectations of the larger Maunsell 4-6-0s. Their performances on the pre-war Bournemouth expresses, as well as on their Hastings hunting grounds and elsewhere, have become legendary. During their last years the 'Schools' were popular for Royal Train workings, always presenting an immaculate spectacle on such occasions.

First of Class Withdrawn: 30919/32 (1961)
Last of Class Withdrawn: 30901/2/3/6/11 /2/5/ 6/21/3/9/30/34–37(1962)
Examples Preserved: 30925/6/8

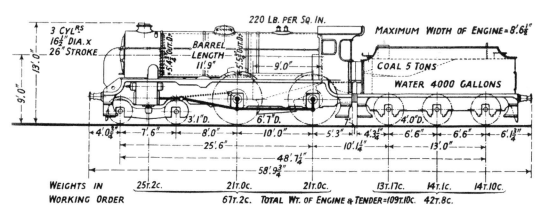

The drawing depicts a 'Schools' class 4-4-0, after the addition of smoke deflectors.

'Schools' class 4-4-0 No. E901 *Winchester*, one of the first batch, without smoke deflectors and with low side window and cutaway to the cab, photographed at Deal in 1931. The class was at its most handsome in this original condition, prior to the addition of deflector plates. The bogie was identical to the 'Lord Nelson' design, with 3 ft 1 in diameter wheels The tender sides were turned in at the top to match the cab profile and permit the engines to run over the Hastings line. In May and June 1931 the new engines commenced running on the Folkestone, Dover and Deal trains, pending Civil Engineering improvements to the Hastings route, to which they were sent in the late summer of the same year. (Ian Allan Library)

In original state, No. E902 *Wellington*, at the head of a Charing Cross–Folkestone–Dover–Ramsgate train, including a Pullman car. The 'Schools' 4-4-0s soon proved their worth on the Kent lines, and put up some astonishing performances for engines of their size. Photographed prior to the fitting of smoke deflectors, which took place in 1932/3. (Ian Allan Library)

When O. V. S. Bulleid succeeded Maunsell as CME of the Southern Railway, he showed a keen interest in the design of the 'Schools' class 4-4-0s, and made footplate runs to study their performance. One outcome of this was the modification of Nos 914/31/7 with Lemaître multiple-jet blast pipes and altered valve ports. At first the chimney fitted was a very clumsy stovepipe affair, as seen here on No. 914 *Eastbourne*, which is finished in Bulleid's experimental light green livery, in 1938. This also shows the enlarged cab side windows and cutaway of the later batches, and the shade fitted around the front cab windows, to protect against soot falling from tunnel roofs. The front window on the driver's side had a wiper and water-spray device fitted. The engine has a speedometer, driven from the rear coupled wheels. (S. C. Townroe Collection)

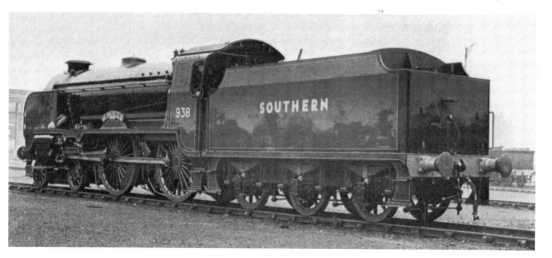

An interesting picture, taken at Eastleigh in 1941 prior to the decision to paint engines in wartime black livery, showing No. 938 *St. Olave's* in a revised style of painting, in Malachite green but with the rear of the tender, front of the cab, and the cylinders in black. Tender lettering I unshaded. Photographed on November 18, 1941, with cab side window glass replaced by steel sheet as an air-raid precaution. Multiple-jet chimney with improved lip appearance. (British Rail SR)

Early in 1948 the newly created nationalised railway system was examining various proposals for a livery and insignia. This bizarre version was exhibited at Waterloo station on March 15, 1948, applied to 'Schools' No. 926 *Repton*, painted in Malachite green SR livery but carrying a huge white totem on the tender side. Happily the scheme was not pursued further, and the engine was quickly despatched to Eastleigh works to have the offending totem erased! (British Rail SR)

From No. 910 onwards, the 4000-gallon tenders of the 'Schools' were of improved design, with a bank of tool and clothes lockers arranged across the footplate, giving better weather protection. A further improvement was made to the tender of No. 932 *Blundells* in 1938, when Eastleigh modified it with higher sides to be self-trimming, in similar fashion to the modified 'Lord Nelson' tenders. This tender remained unique to the class and ran attached to No. 30905 in later days. It is seen here attached to No. 30932, at Bricklayers Arms shed, whilst in early BR hybrid livery scheme of Malachite green with gill sans lettering; circa 1948. (Ian Allan Library)

The choice of LNWR-style lined black livery for the 'Schools' was not altogether a happy one, although they could look smart enough when clean. No. 30919 *Harrow* was photographed at Hildenborough, having just shut off steam for the stop, with the 1.25 pm semi-fast Charing Cross to Tunbridge Wells train, on May 23, 1953. The tender carries the large, original, version of the BR totem, which created quite a pleasing effect. Snifting valves were removed from the smokebox top. (B. E. Morrison)

No. 30922 *Marlborough* is seen in the later version of the lined black livery, with small BR totem on the tender, and modified lining out. The engine makes a fine picture at the head of a train of fitted Continental Train Ferry vans at Bickley Junction on February 20, 1953. The engine retains Maunsell's original single blast pipe and chimney. Only Nos 30900/1/7/9/13–5/7–21/4/9–31/3/4/7–9 were equipped with the Lemaître multiple-jet blast pipe and chimney by Bulleid. (B. E. Morrison)

A welcome decision was the return to green livery for the 'Schools', in later BR steam days, when the dark Brunswick green was applied. No. 30912 *Downside* is seen at Clapham Junction, attached to the eight-wheeled tender from a 'Lord Nelson' class 4-6-0. Two engines ran with these tenders for a while, Nos 30912/21 (from Nos 30865 and 30854 respectively). (M. Edwards)

Section 18

2-6-4T Class W
Goods Tank Engines
Introduced: 1931
Total: 25

A feature of Southern Railway operations in the London area were the freight workings, which included some that were interchanged with the other railways north of the Thames. These were relatively short hauls, but they had to be fitted into the paths available on the suburban electric SR network, without delaying the passenger trains, and once off the third rail they involved lines, which abounded in gradients and curves. These freights were, moreover, often quite heavy loads. To handle this traffic Maunsell designed a three-cylinder tank engine with a high tractive effort and good brake power.

Since the unfortunate episode with the 'River' tanks in 1927, the Southern had produced no steam engines without tenders except the Z class, which were basically for yard service. By reverting to the 2-6-4T wheel arrangement for goods traffic, Maunsell was able to make use of certain parts, such as the side tanks and bogies, which had been discarded when the 'Rivers' were converted to tender engines. The new engines, of Class W, were based upon the three-cylinder N1 class 2-6-0s, and could therefore be described as a goods engine version of the three-cylinder 2-6-4T No. 890 *River Frome*. Although outwardly very similar, the new engines had a different suspension arrangement and method of control for the pony truck and bogie.

The use of three cylinders provided a high and even starting torque, and the braking was made as effective as possible by giving the coupled wheels a high percentage brake force, plus the use of bogie brakes – the latter a feature not often employed on modern British steam engines. The engine brakes were steam operated, but vacuum braking was fitted for use with fitted freight vehicles.

The same design of boiler, with 200 lb psi working pressure, was used as that already fitted to the Class N, N1, U, and U1 2-6-0s, and in due course these boilers were freely interchanged. The heating surface of tubes and flues was 1391 sq. ft and the firebox heating surface was 135 sq. ft, giving a total evaporative heating surface of 1526 sq. ft. The Maunsell superheater had a heating surface of 285 sq. ft, and the grate area was 25 sq. ft.

All three 16.5 by 28 in cylinders drove the centre coupled axle. Tractive effort at 85 per cent of working pressure was 29376 lb. The engines weighed 90.7 tons in full working order, with 2000 gallons of water and 3.5 tons of coal; 63 per cent of the total weight ranked as adhesive.

The engines were built as follows:

| Nos 1911–1915 | Eastleigh | 1932 |
| Nos 1916–1925 | Ashford | 1935/36 |

The first Eastleigh-built batch had the cab arranged for right-hand driving, whereas the Ashford-built engines had left-hand drive. Another difference between the two batches was that Nos 1911–1915 had gravity sanding until 1959/60, when they were converted to steam sanding, which was fitted to the rest of the class from new.

These solid, reliable and handsome tank engines were a daily feature of the London scene for a quarter of a century or more, and they performed their humdrum duties with admirable efficiency.

First of Class Withdrawn: 31923 (1963)
Last of Class Withdrawn: 31914(1964)
None Preserved.

W class 2-6-4T, as built.

The first batch of five locomotives, Nos 1911–1915, were constructed at Eastleigh and entered traffic in SR goods livery of black with green lining and yellow lettering. This batch had right-hand drive and gravity sanding; the sanding was altered to the steam system, under BR auspices, in 1959–60. The London area sheds at Battersea, Norwood and Hither Green received an allocation of W tanks for freight workings.

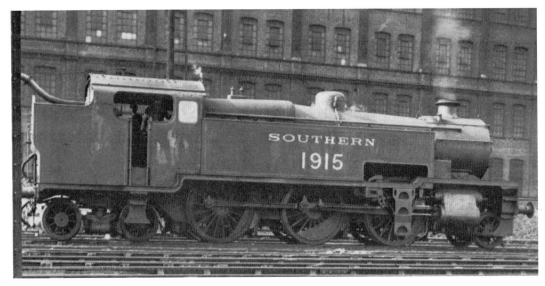

The bogie on the W tanks carried brakes, in order to increase the brake power of these powerful freight locomotives, as can be seen in this study of No. 1915, taken at Stewarts Lane shed on September 15, 1934. The massive set of three footsteps ahead of the cylinders was repeated to the rear, allowing access to the tank fillers. The Ashford batch of engines, Nos 1916–1925, were delivered in plain black livery and the earlier engines were repainted without the green lining in due course. (H. C. Casserley)

A very typical view of a Class W 2-6-4T in operation. No. 31918 eases a train onto the line leading to the West London Extension Railway, at Clapham Junction on June 10, 1962. This was an inter-Regional working, from Norwood Yard to Willesden Junction, the sort of duty the class were designed to handle. The appearance of the engines hardly altered over the years, with only minor changes, such as the removal of the smokebox snifting valves. Livery was always black; only the styles of lettering and insignia varied. The engines were almost exclusively used for freight duties, and the sight of one on empty stock working was a rare delight for the enthusiast. As part of comparative trials, in which LMS type 2-6-4Ts participated, on the Central Section and Eastern Section in May 1948, Class W No. 31918 was selected to work special passenger trains from Ashford to Tonbridge and Victoria to Tunbridge Wells West. Ashford Works had specially prepared the engine for these runs, but no further attempts were made to use the class on passenger turns. (Brian Stephenson)

Section 19

0-6-0 Class Q
Goods Engines
Introduced: 1938
Total: 20

The final design of the Maunsell regime on the Southern Railway did not materialise until after his retirement. In 1938 the first of the Q class 0-6-0s made its appearance from Eastleigh, and Maunsell's successor, O. V. S. Bulleid, is on record as stating that, had he arrived upon the scene earlier, he would have stopped construction of such an uninspired and pedestrian design. This was, perhaps, a rather unfair assessment of Maunsell's engine, which was quite intentionally modest in size and power.

The Southern Railway inherited a number of pre-Grouping 0-6-0 designs, by Stirling, Beattie and others, which it had kept in stock to operate over various secondary routes and branch lines, where larger and more powerful engines were prohibited. These survivors of the Victorian era were showing their age by the mid-1930s and Maunsell produced the Q as an inexpensive modern replacement. The design was not considered as a standard, but it included a good many existing standard parts. It was the first 0-6-0 design to be built for the Southern and it had parts in common with the Class N 2-6-0 and Class L1 4-4-0; the boiler was a smaller version of the L1 boiler, very slightly tapered and with a Belpaire firebox.

A Sinuflo superheater was fitted and these were the only SR engines to be equipped with this pattern of element except for the Lord Nelson class 4-6-0 No. 857 *Lord Howe*. The 21 elements gave a superheated heating surface of 185 sq. ft. The boiler had a heating surface of 1125 sq. ft and the firebox contributed 122 sq. ft, giving an evaporative total of 1247 sq. ft. The grate area was 21.9 sq. ft. The two Ross pop safety valves were set at 200 lb per sq. in working pressure.

Two 19 in by 26 in inside cylinders drove a solid crank axle. Stephenson's link motion, with long-travel piston valves of 10 in diameter were fitted. The valves had outside admission, giving a short and direct passage for the exhaust steam to the blast pipe. The Stirling Ashford steam reverser was fitted, with horizontal cylinders on the left-hand side of the engine.

An indication of the duties envisaged for the Q class can be seen in the very restricted width of only 7 ft 9 in over the cab sides (8 ft 4 in overall) and the total engine weight of no more than 49.5 tons in working order. The maximum axle load was a modest 18 tons, whilst the trailing coupled wheels carried only 13 tons 10 cwt. Tractive effort at 85 per cent working pressure was 26157 lb.

The engines were built as follows:

Nos 530–540   Eastleigh   1938
Nos 541–549   Eastleigh   1939

The first engines constructed had tenders of 3500 gallons, 5 tons coal capacity, off Class U 2-6-0s (which received 4000-gallon tenders); they later received 4000-gallon tenders in some instances. No 545 had a 4000-gallon tender when new.

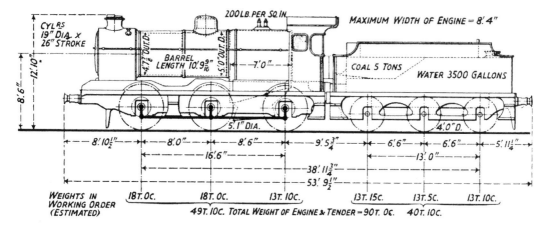

The drawing illustrates the Class Q 0-6-0 design in original condition, with Maunsell chimney and smokebox snifting valves. The front framing is shown as on the prototype No. 530. The remaining engines had the front framing cut away in a concave curve on the upper surface.

The second engine in as-built condition, No. 351, with Maunsell chimney and snifting valves on the smokebox. Entirely in the traditions of the classic British 0-6-0 goods engines, the Q class were neat in appearance and modest in power. They were intended to replace a variety of elderly 0-6-0 types and to be suitable for operation on various secondary routes, including a certain amount of light passenger train work. The Stirling steam reverser fitted to these engines is clearly visible above the centre splasher. (P. F. Winding Collection)

Bulleid had no great liking for the Maunsell Q class and certainly produced a very different locomotive in 1942 in the shape of his own 'Austerity' Q1. Subsequently he attempted to improve the performance of the Maunsell engines by fitting some of them with his multiple-jet blast pipe, together with a rather ugly squat chimney, as seen here on No. 540, photographed passing Oxted with a lightweight goods train. The snifting valves originally fitted have been removed from the smokebox top. (E. R. Wethersett)

In 1955 further attempts were made by BR to improve the draughting of the Q class, and No. 30549 had the Bulleid multiple-jet blast pipe replaced by a new single blast pipe of modified dimensions. At first the engine carried a particularly ugly stovepipe chimney, as seen here. Photographed at Bournemouth Central station on August 28, 1955. A BR standard chimney casting was subsequently fitted. (C. P. Boocock)

From 1960, six more engines of the class had new blast pipes and BR standard chimneys fitted: Nos 30530/6/8/43/5/7. Carrying the BR power classification 4F on the cabside, No. 30543 was photographed shunting in the shed yard at Redhill, in August 1964. The battery box for BR AWS equipment is seen on the platform immediately ahead of the cab.

The BR standard class four chimney certainly suited the Maunsell engines better than the Bulleid multiple-jet application, so far as appearance was concerned. No. 30545 was photographed working hard with a Brighton-bound excursion near Fishergate Halt one hot August day; a reminder of pre-war days, when such excursion abounded on summer weekends, and many humble 'maids-of-all-work' were pressed into service of Britain's coastal resorts. (T. Poulter)

November 1962 saw the first withdrawals of the Q class, and at the same time a number of others were relegated to snow-plough standby duties. No. 30548 was photographed in suitably wintery conditions, at Eastleigh shed on January 5, 1963. The engine replaced the class 700 0-6-0 No. 30316, formerly used, which was withdrawn. (J. C. Haydon)

Appendix 1

The Woolwich Disposals – The Woolworths

Following the Armistice of November 1918, the Government found employment for the staff at the Woolwich Arsenal by placing an order for 100 complete sets of parts for Maunsell Class N 2-6-0s, intended as suitable for national use. As mentioned in the introduction, and in section four, events overtook this policy and the 1923 Grouping created a situation whereby such standard locomotives were not readily accepted. Thus it became necessary to seek buyers further afield. The boilers for most of the engines were constructed by the North British Locomotive Company, but all other parts were made at the munitions factory. The Southern Railway purchased 50 sets of parts and assembled them at Ashford in 1924/5 and this left a further 50 to be disposed of. These were destined (or at least some were) to lead very interesting careers. Right at the end of its existence, the Midland Great Western Railway of Ireland purchased twelve sets of parts at the very low price of £2000 each, and assembled them at their Broadstone Works. The first one appeared very briefly in MGWR livery as their No. 49 (the date of completion was April 9, 1925 by which time the MGWR had been absorbed into the Great Southern Railway) and this was quickly renumbered 410. However, the GSR then decided to buy 15 more, so the numbering was again altered and No. 410 became No. 372. Apart from altering the gauge of the wheels, from 4 ft 8.5 in to the Irish 5 ft 3 in, they were practically identical to the Southern Railway N class engines when new, and the only immediate alteration came about with the last six of the GSR order (which were erected at Inchicore between 1927 and 1930); these had 6 ft instead of 5 ft 6 in driving wheels. The smaller-wheeled variety were Class K1 and were numbered from 372 to 391; those with 6 ft driving wheels were Class K1a and were numbered from 393 to 398. Of the second batch of 15 sets of parts, ordered by the GSR, one set was not erected as a complete locomotive and was kept instead as spares for the rest.

The Metropolitan Railway ordered six sets of parts from Woolwich. The railway was faced with a need for more motive power to handle an expanding suburban goods traffic, and perhaps with Maunsell's own tank engines in mind they produced six exceedingly handsome 2-6-4T locomotives, which bore a strong resemblance to the 'Rivers'. These 2-6-4T goods engines were adapted from the Woolwich N class parts by Mr. G. Hally, the CME of the Metropolitan Railway, and the modifications were carried out by the Newcastle Works of Armstrong Whitworth & Co. Ltd with existing boilers from Robert Stephenson & Co. Darlington, in 1925. They were Class K Nos 111–116.

The disposals listed above involved 33 sets of parts, leaving seventeen, which were incomplete. A rumour was circulated that these sets had been purchased by the Rumanian State Railways and that twelve locomotives had been made from them. This was not the case. All that went to Rumania was a few hundred pounds worth of scrap materials. The remaining parts mostly went to the SR in 1925 and Maunsell obtained some further parts for his EIR tank rebuilds of 1927, which suggests that Woolwich still held stock at that date. In addition to the set of spares held at Inchicore for the K1 and K1a engines, it is believed that the GSR obtained the pony truck and coupled wheels for the solitary PI class 2-6-2T No. 850 from the same source. This suburban tank engine appeared from Inchicore in October 1928.

The nickname Woolworth was often applied to the engines which had originated at Woolwich Arsenal and had subsequently been sold at bargain prices! Certainly, the Irish engines paid for themselves handsomely over the years. An odd end befell three of the Irish locomotives, Nos 391/5/7. In February 1958 they were shipped to Spain, landing at the port of San Juan de Nieva, and ended their lives as raw material for the blast furnaces of Ensidesa Steelworks.

Great Southern Railway of Ireland 2-6-0 No. 376, of the K1 class, in original condition with Maunsell chimney and piston tail rods, in the dull grey livery of the GSR; note tablet exchange equipment on the tender. Except for the widening of the axles to accommodate the 5 ft 3 in gauge, the K1s were virtually identical to the SECR/Southern Railway N class Moguls. (Author's Collection)

In 1945 the Woolwich engines were taken over by CIE, retaining the same numbers. In the severe fuel shortage of 1947 many of them were converted to burn oil, with a large oil tank mounted in the tinder. The smokebox door and the tender sides had large white circles painted on them to denote that the engines were oil-burners, and this indicated to signalmen that they did not require the lengthy fire cleaning stops, then a feature of operations with engines burning poor coal, turf or other inferior fuels. Class K1a 2-6-0 No. 393 is seen here working as an oil-burner, at the head of a Galway train near Liffey Junction, Dublin, in August 1947. Oil firing was abandoned once the coal supply improved and the engines were reconverted accordingly. The six K1a class engines had very small splashers above the running plate, to accommodate the 6 ft diameter driving wheels of this batch.

Class K1 2-6-0 No. 373 in post-war CIE livery of medium green with yellow numerals and insignia, somewhat reminiscent of pre-war Southern Railway days. The engine has a later chimney and a dished smokebox door with a central handwheel and locking pin, in place of the original flat door. The Irish Maunsell 2-6-0s had a reputation for rather rough riding due to inferior maintenance, and had weakened frames, with some stays removed in order to effect weight reduction. Nevertheless they were staunch performers, and a considerable bargain! No. 373 was photographed at Portarlington on an up Thurles–Limerick train on March 19, 1951. (A. Donaldson)

Immaculately clean, No. 383 stands in the yard at Broadstone in July 1956. The tender access ladder was fitted when the engines were converted to oil-burning, and subsequently retained. No smoke deflectors were ever fitted to the Irish engines, and the CIE fitted different chimneys and smokebox doors over the years, as seen here. The engine has tablet changing equipment on the cabside. The piston tail rods were removed from the class in pre-war days, when additional snifting valves were fitted. Seven engines were given extensive overhauls in 1954/5. (C. P. Boocock)

Metropolitan Railway class K 2-6-4T No. 111, the first of six assembled from Woolwich parts and intended for goods traffic, in crimson lake livery. The bunker and trailing bogie design was similar to those of the Metropolitan 4-4-4T passenger tank engines. In Met. days and later, when they carried London Transport livery (1933–1937), they were employed exclusively on fast freights on the Aylesbury line, apart from coming to the rescue of stranded electric trains from time to time. Features of interest were the sliding cab windows, the revised design of the cylinder drain cocks (intended to allow ample clearance over electric conductor rails) and the trip-cock mechanism on the bogie. The odd coincidence of classification – K – the same as the Southern Railway 'Rivers', somehow emphasised their Maunslett origins. The weight in working order was 87 tons 7 cwt and the overall length was 44 ft 10.75 in. (Ian Allan Library)

The large bunker held four tons of coal, and the K 2-6-4Ts carried 2000 gallons of water. With their N class coupled wheels, of 5 ft 6 in diameter (as against the 6 ft of the SR 'Rivers') they were ideal engines for their job and exceedingly handsome to look at. This bunker end view of No. 113 when new is of interest in showing the large numerals used, with the locomotive class painted below. Cabside windows seen in fully opened position. (Ian Allan Library)

In 1937 the LNER took over most of the steam operations on the Metropolitan section of London Transport, including goods working. The six K class 2-6-4Ts were transferred to LNER stock and became class L2, taking the numbers 6158–6163. The fine crimson lake LT livery formerly carried gave way to black and the engines were shedded at the Neasden (GC) depot. After years of freight working they were suddenly placed on passenger turns by their new owners and soon revealed themselves as very capable machines on such work. They were all withdrawn from service in 1947/8, a somewhat premature end to such capable and efficient engines. No. 6162 (formerly No. 115) was photographed at Neasden, still fitted with piston tail rods and snifting valves on the smokebox, although these features were removed from the SR Maunsell engines. (C. C. B. Herbert)

Appendix 2

Miscellaneous Rebuilds

The last 'design' produced by Maunsell in Ireland, before he left Inchicore, was in fact a synthesis of existing parts. The old works shunter was due for renewal and Maunsell replaced it with a 0-4-2ST, named *Sambo*. This had a class 2 4-4-0 boiler. The coupled wheels were those used for existing tank classes. The saddle tank was the same one carried by the former locomotive. *Sambo* appeared in June 1914 and thereafter spent many years shunting at Inchicore. In 1960 it was sent to Amiens Street shed (formerly GNR) where it worked as the Liffey Junction pilot for two years. Withdrawal took place in 1963. The engine is seen shunting at Inchicore on September 20, 1951, by which date it had lost its cabside nameplates and had a later smokebox door. The original smokebox doors were of the double, middle-opening type. (E. M. Patterson)

A wartime need for a powerful shunting locomotive to work at Bricklayers Arms depot was solved by Maunsell by a straight forward conversion. He took Wainwright class C 0-6-0 goods engine and converted it to a 0-6-0 saddle tank, increasing the adhesion weight from 43.75 tons to 53.5 tons. The frames were extended at the rear to accommodate the coal bunker and a fully enclosed cab was fitted. No. 685 appeared from Ashford in 1917, later becoming SR No. 1685, and survived to become BR No. 31685. It was the sole example of class S. (Ian Allan Library)

Drummond had produced five class T14 4-6-0s, numbered 443–447, for the LSWR in 1911. These four-cylinder engines were not entirely successful and Urie subsequently made a number of modifications, including improved lubrication, new fireboxes, extended smokeboxes and Eastleigh superheaters. A persistent cause of trouble were hot boxes and Maunsell attempted to cure this by removing the large splashers (which had led to the engines being nicknamed 'Paddleboxes') and raising the platform over the coupled wheels. He modified the lubrication (fitting mechanical lubricatiors) and fitted the Maunsell pattern superheater with smokebox top snifting valves. No. 460 was the first one dealt with, in 1930, and other engines were similarly modified in the ensuing twelve months or so. No. 443 is seen at Waterloo soon after modification by Maunsell. (P. F. Winding Collection)

By taking spare B4 class boilers and adapting the Marsh LBSCR class I1 4-4-2T to carry them, Maunsell produced the I1X class of twenty engines, which were a considerable improvement upon the originals. Rebuilding took place over the period 1925–1932 and prolonged the useful life of these Central Section branch line passenger engines. The B4 boiler was an excellent saturated-steam boiler, displaced from the B4 4-4-0s when they were converted to B4X superheated engines. (Ian Allan Library)

In 1927 a requirement for heavier and more powerful branch line engines for some of the West of England branches (where the permissible axle load had been raised to 16 tons, by reconstruction) was met by the rebuilding of existing Stroudley LBSCR class E1 0-6-0Ts. A number of these were surplus to requirements and Maunsell was able to reduce their axle loading to suit the new requirement by converting them to 0-6-0Ts, adding a pony truck at the rear, beneath an extended coal bunker. A smart little engine resulted, with a neat cab and bunker, and vacuum brakes instead of air. Two were dealt with at first, found to be successful, and a further eight were authorised. They worked on a number of West Country branches, surviving into BR ownership. EIR class No. 2608, illustrated here, was formerly LBSCR No. 108 *Jersey*. The pony trucks were obtained from the Woolwich N class 2-6-0 stock of spare parts. (Ian Allan Library)

When electrification displaced the massive Billinton LBSCR 4-6-4Ts from the Central Section, Maunsell converted them to tender engines for use on the Western Section, and attached them to 5000-gallon Urie bogie tenders. Classified N15X, the rebuild were graceful engines but lacked the sparkle of the 'King Arthurs'. Only slight alterations were made to the engines; in particular, the boiler pressure was increased from 175 lb per sq. in to 180, and the cylinders were lined to 21 in diameter. In wartime black livery, No. 2328 *Hackworth* is seen on a Salisbury stopping train at Winchfield in May 1947. During World War II some of them were loaned to the Great Western Railway for freight service. (M. W. Earley)

SR 'Lord Nelson' class 4-6-0 No. E860 *Lord Nelson*, posed for the publicity camera, showing the small oval numberplate on the cabside, the E prefix to the number, and the design of the nameplates mounted on the centre splasher. (Ian Allan Library)

Bibliography

The reader seeking further information about the locomotives of R. E. L. Maunsell, and their performance in everyday service, is recommended to the following works, which the present author found invaluable during compilation of this pictorial history:

Bradley, D. L. *Locomotives of the South Eastern and Chatham Railway*. Railway Correspondence and Travel Society.

Bradley, D. L. *Locomotives of the London and South Western Railway*. Railway Correspondence and Travel Society.

Bradley, D. L. *Locomotives of the Southern Railway*. Part 1. Railway Correspondence and Travel Society

Donaldson/McDonnell/O'Neill. *A Decade of Steam*. Railway Preservation Society of Ireland.

Nock, O. S. *Maunsell Locomotives*. Edward Everard.

Nock, O. S. *Southern Steam*. David & Charles.

Townroe, S. C. *The Arthurs, Nelsons and Schools of the Southern*. Ian Allan Ltd.

A wealth of information is contained within the pages of the following journals, for the more diligent reader:

The Locomotive Magazine.
The Railway Gazette.
The Railway Magazine.
Trains Illustrated.
Modern Transport.
The Railway Observer.
The SLS Journal.

A companion volume, *Bulleid Locomotives*, by Brian Haresnape completes the Pictorial History of Southern Railway steam locomotive design, from the retirement of R. E. L. Maunsell until the end of steam. (Published by Ian Allan Ltd.)